C000259702

IRISH PUBS

Barrie Pepper

Eric Dobby Publishing

Published by
Eric Dobby Publishing Ltd
All enquiries for rights to
12 Warnford Road, Orpington, Kent BR6 6LW, UK

© 1998 Barrie Pepper

A catalogue record is available for this book from the British Library.

ISBN: 1 85882 046 4

Printed in Hong Kong

CONTENTS

A traditional Irish cottage in Bunratty Folk Park

MAP OF IRELAND

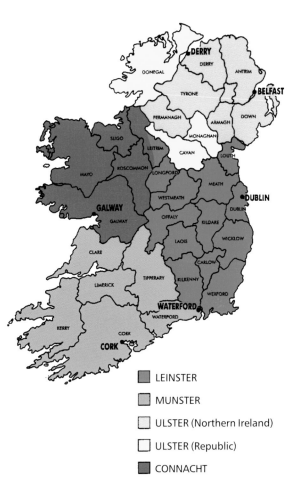

THE AUTHOR

Barrie Pepper is one of the best known writers on pubs and the brewing industry and he has ten books to his credit including the recently published *International Book of Beer*. For the past seven years he has been Chairman of the British Guild of Beer Writers and he is the founder Chairman of the International Federation of Beer Writers. He is also an experienced travel writer and broadcaster and has written much about Ireland over the past 25 years. This book presents his favourite pubs out of the many he has visited in a quarter of a century love affair with the island of Ireland. He stresses that they are entirely a personal choice.

THE IRISH PUB

Nowhere in the world are there pubs as idiosyncratic as those in Ireland. Their uniqueness makes them much admired and they are universally copied. But however many attempts are made to recreate the archetypal Irish pub in such places as England, Scotland, Spain, the United States and even Japan the imitators are seeking the impossible. Irish bars they may call themselves with Irish folk behind them and even Irish drinks sold over them but Irish they are not and never will be.

An Irish pub cannot be built from bricks and mortar. It has to be created, moulded and lovingly assembled over many years, centuries even. And the longevity of an Irish public house is often matched by the longevity of the family that runs it. Irish pub-owning families count their occupation of licensed premises in centuries rather than decades. The atmosphere is something that develops slowly rather than by adding a coat of paint here or knocking a wall out there. It comes from the people who run the pub and those that drink in it.

Essentially the Irish pub is a place to drink in. Its development is such that many have taken on other purposes. The rural beerhouse could not subsist on its own account and another function, usually that of a village shop, was necessary for survival. John Millington Synge in his play *The Playboy of the Western World* creates the perfect image. He calls it 'Country public house or shebeen' and gives the first actor the job of making out the weekly order: '...six yards of stuff to make a yellow gown. A pair of lace boots with lengthy heels on them and brassy eyes. A hat is suited for a wedding day. A fine tooth comb. To be sent with three barrels of porter...'

The description 'bar and grocery' remains commonplace in country Ireland even to this day. And such trades as undertaker, tailor, even coal merchant and estate agent are carried on alongside that of publican. In cities it is a different matter. Pubs are the centre of commercial life and often the place where the working man, of whatever class, eats at lunch time and where deals were struck and trysts contemplated if not achieved.

But, whatever the ancillary purpose, it is the business of selling drink that is all important. And for most of the pubs in Ireland - in the Republic or the north - that means principally Guinness stout. The honourable exception being Cork where the city has two stout breweries - Beamish & Crawford, and Murphy's - of its own.

Arthur Guinness bought his Dublin brewery in 1759 but it was not until 1796 that he started brewing porter - a forerunner of stout. Stout, it was said, was a stouter version of porter. Porter took its name from its popularity with the porters and humpers of the London markets where it was first brewed in 1722. There were older breweries in Ireland and others had brewed porter before Arthur Guinness but his was the success story, the Irish dream, and despite a few dips in the nineteenth century the Guinness brewery grew to become the largest in the world. Guinness became the name of a drink in its own right and its association with Ireland and the city of Dublin is now well established. When Brendan Behan heard someone say that the Guinness family had always been very good to the people of Dublin he responded by saying that the people of Dublin are very kind to the Guinnesses.

Ireland's other pub drink is whiskey, spelled and produced differently than the Scottish version. Irish whiskey is distilled three times which ensures the maximum purity of spirit and no other whiskey in the world is distilled more than twice. It is claimed that whiskey reached Ireland as far back as the sixth century and today Old Bushmills in County Antrim which dates from 1608 is the oldest working distillery in the world.

There are of course other Irish drinks. Irish ale with its reddish glow and malty taste is brewed in Belfast , Lisburn and Kilkenny. And, surprisingly in Paris, Amsterdam and Colorado too for Letts of Enniscorthy in County Wexford which ceased brewing its George Killian Ale in 1956 now licences three foreign breweries to do so. Cask conditioned or real ale is rare in Ireland although there has been a renaissance recently particularly in the pubs of Northern Ireland.

There are also cream liqueurs with a whiskey base of which Baileys is the best known and its remarkable success is such that it accounts for one per cent of all Irish exports. And, of course, there is *poitín* (pronounced, roughly, potcheen), mountain dew, moonshine, call it what you will. It is a drink full of romance mainly because of its illegality and tales of distilling it in the distant hills of the west. Today a legal still operates at Bunratty in County Clare but its product is not sold in Irish pubs and is only allowed for export.

And today pubs in Ireland are good for food. Ten years ago it was difficult to obtain much more than a sandwich or a bowl of soup in most of them. Now the demand for quality has brought a revolution in food. Many pubs have imaginative menus with substantial meals typical of the Irish style with imagination and good quality ingredients merging together.

The other speciality of the Irish pub that has helped develop its unique character is music. Some make a great scene of it, others play the low key but most have at least one night each week when a local group will play traditional music to enthusiastic drinkers.

Irish pubs range in style from the wonderful high Victorian gin palaces of downtown Dublin and Belfast to the tiny shebeens of the western counties. They offer varying levels of comfort and service. Some are essentially for locals, others are developed simply to attract the visitor yet most have a friendly atmosphere and characteristics that could not be other than Irish. The Irish pub is clearly identifiable and firmly implanted in the world's drinking culture. If it were not so then so many other nations would not try to copy it. And fail.

ACKNOWLEDGEMENTS

Thanks are due to John Lahiffe of the Irish Tourist Board for his help in providing me with useful contacts; to Colin Maddox of Kershaw Public Relations for arranging visits to Ireland with Irish Ferries; to Brian Houston and Lesley Allman of Bass Brewers for arranging a visit to Northern Ireland; to Jim Scanlon and Jack Thompson who were wonderful companions and critics, to Chris Clarken for talking to me over a pint or two or three; to Mark and Eleanor for their patience and help; to J J Tohill for sharing his knowledge of pubs in Northern Ireland and a number of other folk, particularly licensees, who have helped me sometimes without realising it by allowing me to pick their brains. And to my dear wife Carolynne for driving me all over Ireland on the pretext of taking a holiday. I must emphasise the point that while I sought advice on which pubs to include in this guide the final choice was entirely mine. It may upset some folk but so be it, they, like me, can hope for a second edition.

PICTURE CREDITS

Many of the pictures were supplied by the licensees or owners of the pubs concerned. Those on pages 130, 132, 133 and 134 were by Mark Hutchinson and on pages 27, 30, 34, 35, 44, 51, 57, 59, 65, 70, 78 and 98 by Jim Scanlon. The rest were by the author.

USING THIS GUIDE

The pubs included in this guide are divided into two sections - the Republic of Ireland and Northern Ireland and in each section they are set out in alphabetical order, first by county, then by town and finally by pub. A third section gives information about those breweries and distilleries and other centres connected with the drink trade that allow visitors.

A telephone number, where available, is given for each entry in the form that a call would be made from the country in which it is located. To make a call to the Republic of Ireland from Northern Ireland or from most other nations you omit the first figure '0' and prefix the number with 00 353. So a number in the guide that reads: 071 70933 would be dialled: 00 353 71 70933. To dial an entry in Northern Ireland from the Republic or another country use a similar system with the international code for Britain of 00 44. For example 01232 325368 would be dialled 00 44 1232 325368.

Try also entries are usually other pubs in the locality and those marked qv (quod vide) are also in the guide. Occasionally restaurants are included.

See also entries are places worth visiting in the area. They are simply a few ideas and are not intended to take the place of a good guide book.

LORD BAGENAL INN

Just off the N9 Waterford to Carlow road, in Leighlinbridge, Co Carlow
Tel: 0503 21668

The *Lord Bagenal* is a Tardis. It has a wonderfully old-fashioned and tiny original pub front in the village's main street but around the back in its spacious car park is the modern bit with loads of room in both bar and restaurant. Its main purpose is food which is excellent with lots of Irish specialities including local cheeses and seafood. Bar food is served all day. The wine list is extensive and reasonably priced and the stout is beautifully kept. Children are made welcome here - there is a special menu for them - and there is a playground nearby. Leighlinbridge is prettily situated on the River Barrow and is in good climbing and walking country and a good stopping place on north-south (and reverse) motor runs.

See also: 12th century Black Castle (in the village).

MONK'S PUB

West end of the village on the coast road, Ballyvaughan, Co Clare
Tel: 065 77059

This is a tremendously popular pub in a busy holiday village. Roads
from Ballyvaughan run either by an attractive route to Galway, south
through the natural history delights of the Burren or by the coast
road to the magnificent Cliffs of Moher. *Monk's Pub* is on this latter
road at the edge of the village just opposite the pier and is a great
stopping off place. There always seems to be something happening
here if the crowds are anything to go by; perhaps it's the excellent
setting of the place which is matched by the first class facilities
within. The pub is comfortable and welcoming with a myriad of
small rooms, open fires (when necessary), a great pint of stout and
home-made meals in which local sea food predominates. This is a
great pub for families with two large dining tables in the main bar.
But, if the sun shines, the favourite spot is the beer garden to watch
the antics of the canoeists and the water skiers in Ballyvaughan Bay
which is a child of Galway Bay.

Try also: *O'Loughlin's* in the village and the *An Féar Gorta* tea
rooms.

See also: Aillwee Cave, the Burren and the Cliffs of Moher.

DURTY NELLY'S

Next to the castle in Bunratty, Co Clare
Tel: 061 364861

Durty Nelly's is one of the best known pubs in Ireland. It stands next to the imposing Bunratty castle, a Norman tower built by the O'Briens, one of the great families of Ireland, and Bunratty Folk Park where recreations of houses and farms of the region down the ages and through the classes are on view. The pub is always thronged with drinkers, although some are merely voyeurs who have come to see why it has such a name. It is a relatively modern tale and was titled as such after some soldiers saw a rat run across the bar: 'this is a real dirty Nelly's,' one said. And it stuck. The pub dates back 150 years when it was known as *The Pike* but its origins are in the early seventeenth century when it was built as a toll house. There is plenty of traditional music here both in organised and casual sessions. This is the quintessential Irish pub with its many rooms and bars, two restaurants, sawdust on the floors and all the qualities that you would expect of such a place. Pints of great distinction flow as briskly here as the mighty Shannon River just across the main Limerick to Ennis highway. The stream alongside *Durty Nelly's* is the River Ratty trailing its way from the hills of Clare to join Ireland's longest river. The pub is well sited and on warm evenings it is ideal for outdoor drinking. You can watch the transatlantic flights take off from Shannon or just look around you. Food is eclectic from simple sandwiches in the bars to gourmet banquets in the Loft restaurant.

Try also: *Mac's* pub in the folk park (free admission in the evening) and Bunratty Winery - Ireland's only legal *poitín* distillery.

See also: Bunratty Castle and Folk Park.

O'CONNOR'S PUB

Doolin, County Clare
In the centre of the village just off the L54 road from Lahinch to
Ballyvaughan
Tel: 065 74168

Doolin and Gus O'Connor's pub are synonymous. The pub's
reputation for folk music stretches across the world and most of the
best musicians have played here at some time in their career; many
of their photographs decorate the walls. The popularity of
O'Connor's has led to extensions over the years but there is still a
homely atmosphere which stems from the style of the place - a small
grocery by the entrance and a hotch-potch of rooms and spaces
served from the one bar. And usually by one of the family. Gus is the
seventh generation to have run the pub since the O'Connors acquired
it in 1832. He looks set to do so for some time yet although there are
sons in the offing. The food is substantial with such offerings as Irish
Stew, and reasonably priced too. The drink goes down well with
most people opting for stout although Irish Coffee is very popular.
But it will be the music that the cosmopolitan crowd are there for.
Young and old, Irish and foreigner, back packer or chauffeur driven;
they all head for *O'Connor's* and they are not disappointed. In this
comfortable, often crowded and unpretentious pub there is music
every night of the week and on Sunday lunchtimes and oft times
between. If not in the pub then across the road where there are a few
tables, a wall to sit on and a stream to contemplate. Up the road
where the wild Atlantic roars is the ferry stage for the Aran Islands,
a throwback to the thirties and a fascinating day out. (See also
Galway - Inisheer). Doolin is a great place for camping and there are
several well run hostels.

Try also: *McGann's Pub, James Cullinan's* restaurant and
guesthouse.

See also: The Aran Islands, the Cliffs of Moher, the Burren.

BROGAN'S

O'Connell Street in the town centre of Ennis, Co Clare
Tel: 065 29480

There is always a sense of urgency about *Brogan's* pub situated as it is in one of Ennis's busiest shopping streets. It has a long bar and comfortable settled alcoves opening off the main room where waiters dash here and there and at lunchtimes the place has a slight touch of disorder that is reminiscent of a Dublin city centre pub. Brothers Seamus and Paddy Brogan attract a good cross section of Ennis life to their pub and restaurant as well as many visitors. The bar and its backdrop is particularly attractive; all dark wood and mirrors with trade signs and posters of local events. Busy, in every way. The food is great and there is always lots of it whether it be a sandwich or their wonderful home-made hamburgers (with three vegetables). There is also a restaurant at the front and another on the first floor where the steaks are wonderful. In the pub you can sit at the bar on high stools, perch on buffets at low tables or luxuriate on settles in an alcove and enjoy a pint. You will be well served and well satisfied.

Try also: *The Usual Place* (qv) and *The Cloisters*.

See also: Ennis cathedral.

THE USUAL PLACE

Market Place, Ennis, Co Clare
Tel: 065 20512

It makes a claim to be the oldest pub in Ennis although I doubt it had this name when it first opened its doors to customers. *The Usual Place* is, to say the least, an unusual name for a pub, it could be unique. But it does make sense: 'see you in the usual place' is one way of saying to those in the know where you are off to yet keeping others in the dark. In such a way pubs in England are sometimes called 'The Church' or 'The Post Office'. The attraction of the stone and brick-built exterior are reflected inside with a small bar reeking atmosphere and friendliness. There are old posters, photographs and mirrors on the walls and a museum-like exhibition of ancient agricultural implements. A most unusual wooden spiral staircase adds to the pub's character. It is a pub for conversation and there is always plenty to talk about. The setting of *The Usual Place* is ideal in a broad street leading off Ennis's Market Place, once called The Mall, now Lower Market Street, it is at the heart of Ennis. The county town of Clare is the perfect place to centre a holiday with so many attractions within easy reach: the River Shannon and its lakes, the Burren, coastal resorts and the eastern mountains; and the town itself is full of interest with a distinct personality all its own.

Try also: *Brogan's* (qv) and *The Cloisters*.

See also: Ennis Friary, the de Valera museum.

THE ARCHWAY

New Town Street (centre of village), Ennistymon, Co Clare
Tel: 065 71080

Ennistymon is a town so full of shops and pubs that it makes you wonder where their customers live. Perhaps they sell to one another. In any book, guide or poster on Ireland it's almost certain that there will be one photograph of an Ennistymon shop or pub front, if not several. *The Archway* is regularly found in these publications not least because of its position as the entrance to the famous cascades on the River Inagh (or is it the River Cullenagh? Never trust an Irish Ordnance Survey map!) The falls roar when in flood and are placidity itself in drought. At one time their force ran a small electric power station that fed the Falls Hotel. Viewing from the special platform is a must, particularly during the salmon run. And then to *The Archway* for refreshment. It is an all-purpose pub with drink, food, accommodation and entertainment. And fabulous views too which ought to go without saying. Like several others in Ennistymon this is a favourite pub for musicians and many of the country's best play here. There are traditional sessions here every night in summer and at weekends in winter.

Try also: *Joe McHugh's* at Liscannor, Unglert's bakery for some of best home-baked bread and confectionery in Ireland (closed Mondays).

See also: The cascades.

NAGLE (EUGENE'S)

Main Street, Ennistymon, Co Clare
Tel: 065 71777

What appears to be at first sight a tiny comfortable pub stretches back further than you think with several nooks and crannies. It stands out on Ennistymon's main street which is full of pubs. At one time this small town claimed to have more pubs for its population than any other in the British Isles. It may still have and what are still there, and there are plenty, are an eclectic lot. *Nagle's* is for music as are several others whereas another *Nagle* is also an undertaker and *Griffin* sells black coal as well as black stout. Many famous musicians have played here and their pictures and posters adorn the walls. There is a tiny stage for the performers although spontaneous bursts of music may sound out from all parts of the pub. If the music is not live then it will be the best quality recorded sound from The Chieftains to Wolfgang Amadeus Mozart. The Guinness is great here as is the coffee.

Try also: A walkabout on Main Street where there may be a handful of pubs providing music all on the same evening. At Inagh, seven miles along the Ennis road is the Biddy Early brewery serving a pub of the same name - this is first brewery to be opened in County Clare for many years and the stout is cask conditioned - unique in Ireland.

See also: The cascades and the amazing variety of shops for such a small town.

PEPPER'S BAR

East end of the village, Feakle, Co Clare
Tel: 061 924131

Gary (no relation to the editor!) is the third generation of Peppers to run this pub and his ancestors have been here since 1810 when the McGinnis family were the tenants. This attractive roadside pub on the edge of the village of Feakle is devoted to folk music. It plays an important part in the annual Feakle Folk Music Festival every August at which many well known Irish and international artists take part, including Seane Keane and Matt Molloy (see Westport, County Mayo) of The Chieftains, Frankie Gavin and Liam O'Flynn. It even has its own mini-festival in December - Pepper's Christmas Capers. The bar is stone flagged and its walls display many photographs of folk musicians taken in the pub. It is cosy and comfortable and little has changed over the years. Next to it is a large concert room with its own bar and there is also a small walled garden with seats and tables where an open air concert is held on the June bank holiday weekend. The food at *Pepper's* is simple enough with Guinness stew and roast chicken and other straightforward cooked dishes, but the best value here are the sandwiches - try the home roasted ham with slices half an inch thick. The drink, ubiquitous Guinness stout, is in fine form.

See also: The lakes and hills of east Clare - quite beautiful and a fisherman's paradise.

VAUGHAN'S

West end of the village, Kilfenora, Co Clare
Tel: 065 88004

Kilfenora is an attractive village at the gateway to the Burren, a vast limestone region of great geological and archeological interest that stretches across the north-west of County Clare. Amongst its many treasures are an ancient cathedral with some magnificent high crosses, the Burren Display Centre and a clutch of good pubs including one in which you can get measured for a suit. *Vaughan's* is the livestock market pub and very much the sort of place you will want to return to. There is a general atmosphere of well-being and friendliness there whatever the time or season. But Monday lunchtimes in particular are great when the sheep market takes place in the yard behind the pub and farmers treat themselves to enormous helpings of bacon and cabbage or Irish stew and encourage visitors to do likewise. Take the hint. There is plenty going on here and much room to do it in. The bar is L-shaped and serves a small comfortable lounge at the front and a larger bar area. The newly opened Parlour Restaurant is in what, until recently, was the Vaughan family living quarters. It concentrates on dishes made with ingredients garnered locally. At the back is a delightful garden with views over the Burren hills and swings and the like for the kids. A converted thatched barn is the scene for barbecues, set dancing and music sessions - the Kilfenora Ceili Band has won many prizes. Kilfenora, like Rome, has the Pope as its Bishop. Ask about it!

Try also: *Nagle's* (lounge bar and outfitters).

See also: The high crosses of Kilfenora, Burren Display Centre.

PERCY FRENCH BAR

Moore Street, Kilrush, Co Clare
Tel: 065 51615

Kilrush was a terminus for the much-loved, often abused but sorely missed West Clare Railway. The 3-feet gauge trains ran from Ennis to the coast at Lahinch and then south to the twin resorts of Kilkee and Kilrush. In 1896 Percy French, the song writer and entertainer, failed to arrive for a concert in Kilkee because of a breakdown of one of the West Clare engines. He sued the railway company for loss of earnings and damage to his reputation and won. What's more he also wrote a satirical and very popular song: *Are ye right there, Michael?* in which the company got the full benefit of his astringent wit:

> You may talk of Columbus's sailing
> Across the Atlantical sea
> But he never tried to go railing
> From Ennis as far as Kilkee.
> You run for the train in the mornin',
> The excursion train starting at eight,
> You're there when the clock gives a warnin'
> And there for an hour you'll wait.

And so on through a catalogue of errors until it concludes:

> And as you're wobbling through the dark,
> You hear the guard make this remark:

"Are you right there Michael?, are you right?
Do you think that ye'll be home before its light?
'Tis all dependin' whether
The ould engine holds together -
And it might now, Michael, so it might!"

French's reputation (and his many songs) is evergreen in south Clare and this pub is a shrine to his memory in the way he would have wanted it. It is large and popular on a shopping street that runs eastwards from the main square. There is a small select bar at the front with a piano (rare in Ireland) and a larger lounge bar at the rear. The walls are decorated with murals celebrating Percy French and also the delights of the area. There is music three times each week with, no doubt, some of the master's songs. There is another *Percy French Bar* in Newcastle, Co Down.

Try also: *Taylor's Bar* in Moyasta for memorabilia of the West Clare Railway.

See also: Cappagh pier and marina and Scattery Island.

GALVIN'S

South end of Main Street next to the church, Lahinch, Co Clare
Tel: 065 81045

Galvin's (which is often called *Comber's* after the family that owned it for many years) has the unique distinction of being the only pub in Ireland that is semi-detached from a church. It all stems from the time when a former owner sold a small plot of land to the Roman Catholic church next door to allow a small extension and now the two village essentials are enjoined. The pub, which has a commanding view of the always crowded main street, dates from around 1780 when it was built as a coaching inn. The original arches are still there. There is a small front snug which should seat about 15 people but often holds 40. Opposite is a longer, more open room and this large bar area and lounge is where the live music sessions take place. These are usually organised by the owner, John Galvin, but many are impromptu with well known artists taking part. Sean Keane of The Chieftains is a frequent visitor and the flute player P J Crotty lives in the village. John Galvin bought the pub from the Comber family in 1986; he has made some alterations but the essential character remains. It is a drinkers' house although simple food is available. In late August the literati, politicians and intelligentsia of Ireland descend on Lahinch and make Galvin's their headquarters. They are there for the Merriman literary summer school which has gained the title: 'A lark in the Clare air'.

Try also: *Kenny's* (qv) and the *Atlantic* and *Aberdeen Arms* hotels.

See also: Lahinch championship golf courses, the Cliffs of Moher and the Burren.

KENNY'S

Main Street, Lahinch, Co Clare
Tel: 065 81433

This is a very popular family-run pub in the centre of this small but busy seaside resort on the Atlantic coast that is sometimes called 'Limerick-on-sea' because of its affinity with the folk of that city. Invariably the staff behind the bar are members of the Kenny family usually led by the owner Donal Kenny himself. If the sons and daughters are not around then they will probably be in one of the other family businesses; the woollen goods and souvenir shop across the street or at the factory in nearby Miltown Malbay. An island bar serves this large pub where the stout is fine and the *craic* is great. It has a high reputation for bar meals, particularly sea food, with remarkably generous portions. Occasional sessions of traditional folk music are held in the summer months and bed and breakfast is available.

Try also: *Galvin's* (qv), *Frawley's* and *Mr Eamon's* restaurant.

See also: Seaworld on the promenade.

IRISH ARMS

On the road leading north out of the Square in Lisdoonvarna, Co Clare
Tel: 065 74207

Lisdoonvarna is Ireland's premier spa with both sulphur and iron springs. It is also in the centre of the Burren and a very useful centre for touring the counties of Clare and Galway. Its other claim to fame is that it is the matchmaker's town and in Autumn there is a festival at which, it is said, American spinsters and widows seek out rich, Irish bachelor farmers. Or Irish bachelor farmers seek out rich American widows. Whatever, it is an occasion for lots of joviality and the hotels and pubs stay open most of the night. But there is plenty more to do and see here. Try the *Irish Arms* at the north end of town next to the Post Office and you'll find a good deal going on whatever the season. It is a solid symmetrical building with an interesting interior that allows disparate groups to enjoy the atmosphere without too much interference. It is a comfortable pub with wooden-backed settles and stools at the bar. Yet it can operate as a whole, such as when folk music nights are held. There is a small stage and dance floor. The food is excellent and substantial with Beef in Guinness particularly popular; naturally it must be accompanied by a pint of stout. There is an interesting set of photographs of old Lisdoonvarna on the walls as well as some interesting prints of the Aran islands by a local artist, John Shelton.

Try also: *Roadside Tavern.*

See also: Spa Wells Centre, Spectacle Bridge, Ballynalacken Castle.

ANCHOR TAVERN

New Street, Bantry, Co Cork
Tel: 027 50012

The Anchor stands out in a town full of pubs. And there is great rivalry between them so much so that a notice in the Anchor warns: 'No obscene language, particularly such words as (and then follows a list of many of the other pubs in Bantry.)' This eccentric pub is full of memorabilia mainly to do with sailors and the sea and lots of amusing notices penned by the landlord himself. Its justly famous home-smoked mackerel is served with horseradish sauce and the advice: 'You no lika, you no paya'. Three different stouts are served; this being County Cork where two of them - Beamish & Crawford's and Murphy's - are brewed and, of course, there is the ubiquitous Guinness. The place is full of character and characters including the present owner Bill O'Donnell. On weekday mornings a crossword club meets here over a drink. *The Anchor* tavern is in the centre of Bantry no more than a good hit with a hurling stick from the bustling harbour.

Try also: All the other obscenely named pubs in the town!

See also: Bantry House (a stately home in which reasonably priced accommodation is available), Glengarrif and Garinish Island.

AN SPAILPÍN FÁNAĊ

South Main Street, in Cork city centre
Tel: 021 277949

You can be sure of a good pint of Beamish in this pub for it is situated opposite the brewery. In fact all three national stouts are available as well as lagers and an interesting new drink called Beamish Red. It is in the same style as several other beers around which are basically ales with a stout consistency and head and served cool as a lager. Try them now for I fear they may not have the longevity of stouts. However back to *An Spailpín Fánac* which means 'the wandering labourer' which is a most appropriate name for a downtown pub. It is just the place to rest one's weary bones after a day's hard work. A frame on the wall explains all provided you can read Irish.

There is one long bar with a number of separate drinking areas including a tiny snug with its own access to the bar - ideal for business meetings or lovers' trysts. The walls are of uncovered brick with wooden panelling. The food here is straightforward and reasonably priced and includes such Irish standards as bacon and cabbage and Irish stew and some good value sandwiches. There is a restaurant on the first floor. Traditional music is played on several nights. The pub dates back to 1779 and has one of the longest continuous licences in Cork City.

Try also: *Reidy's Wine Vaults* (qv), *Le Château* (qv).

See also: Jameson Whiskey Heritage Centre, Midleton.

CANTY'S

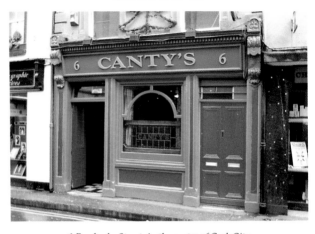

6 Pembroke Street, in the centre of Cork City
Tel: 021 270566

Until 100 years ago this was *The Star Hotel* and then it was bought by the Canty family who ran it as a bar, with the present owner taking over in 1978. Barry Buttimer is well known throughout Ireland mainly because of his work with the Vintners' Federation of Ireland of which he is President. He also has other claims to fame including the Distinguished Flying Cross which he won whilst serving with the United States Air Force in Vietnam. He is also a propagandist for better quality service and proves it every day with the style with which he runs his pub. The entrance to *Canty's* is not very prepossessing but its comforts inside make up for that. It is probably the most cosmopolitan pub in Cork City serving as it does a mixture of folk ranging from solicitors to street sweepers and including all age groups. This, by Barry's own lead, is a first name pub. He is a big man and the pub he runs is big too, not so much in size as in quality.

Try also: *Henchy's* (qv), *Le Chateau* (qv), the *Old Reliable* in Shandon Street.

See also: Several great churches and attend a rake of festivals: film, jazz and pop.

HENCHY'S

40/41 St Luke's Cross, Cork City
Tel: 021 501115

The handsome green sign board of *Henchy's* proclaims: 'Tea and wine merchants' and here we have yet another fine example of the idiosyncratic Irish pub which combines several functions in the one establishment. Henchy's dates from 1884 and the family has remained in charge ever since. In that time the pub will have seen plenty of history. The great short story writer and translator Frank O'Connor lived as a boy in nearby Harrington Square during the early years of this century. Not too far away lived his friend and another master of the short story, Sean O'Faolain. The north side of the republic's second city is dominated by Shandon Church and its famous bell tower with wonderful views from which no doubt a fine snapshot of *Henchy's* can be obtained. Enter it: store to the right, bar to the left and a room shaped like a dog's hind leg. There is also a snug which can be kept private by drawing curtains across. The decor is plain but there is a surfeit of attractive stained glass in windows and doors. Here you will find a great pint of both Cork stouts - Beamish & Murphy - as well as Guinness. Bar food is available all day. In front of the pub is a green painted kiosk which many folk remember newspapers being sold from although its original purpose was as a toll booth to catch the unwary countrymen coming down the hill into the city.

Try also: *Canty's* (qv), *Old Reliable* in Shandon Street.

See also: Shandon church with its famous bells.

LE CHÂTEAU

Patrick Street, in the centre of Cork City
Tel: 021 270370

This is the only pub in Cork's premier shopping street - in fact it has entrances in three different streets - and it stands out not just because of this but for its fine narrow facade which is most attractive and in summer is always florally decorated. It takes its name from the fact that it is in what was once the Huguenot quarter of the city where, in the eighteenth century, French merchants lived. There are two bars on the ground floor and a function room upstairs. The bars are separate and evolve from different licences. *Reidy's* (the owner's family name) is at the rear and has its own entrance; it is all dark wood and old glass and very atmospheric with a long polished bar that came from the *Peel Hotel* in Leeds when it closed twenty years ago. *Keiley's*, which is entered from Patrick Street, is similar in many ways but much airier and lighter. There is a connecting way between the two to allow visitors to choose which bar appeals to them. The food is important here with sea food predominating on the menu. There is a good range of drinks with a fine choice of whiskey and whisky.

Try also: *The Long Valley* in Winthrop Street, *Reidy's Wine Vaults* (qv) which is owned by the same family.

See also: Crawford Art Gallery in Emmet Place, the view from Shandon Church.

REIDY'S WINE BAR

Lancaster Quay, on the N22 Killarney Road, in the west end of Cork City
Tel: 021 275751

This is a bar of great quality that dates from 1835. The attractive red brick entrance is in complete contrast to the interior which is a delight. The tiled hall way leads you into a cathedral-like vaulted room that has been carefully converted from a wine warehouse - hence the name. Wine is sold here but not to the exclusion of beers and spirits. A long curved bar sets off the room with its brass foot rail and stylish high-backed stools and an imposing bar back with mirrors and a London clock. Tall screens of polished wood and good etched glass divide the room effectively and a tiled snug with its own door and access to the bar offers the ultimate in privacy and comfort. Old trade mirrors add to the pleasure and cartoons by Hynes give a touch of humour. A minstrels' gallery overlooks all this. The food is excellent with meals served well into the evening.

This is a delightful pub once named 'Irish Black and White Pub of the Year' and it is conveniently situated opposite *Jury's Hotel* and in the heart of small hotel and bed and breakfast territory. The Reidy family remain in charge with sisters Maura Reidy and Ann Green controlling the bar and Noelle Reidy (a sister-in-law) overlooking the catering and even baking the bread.

Try also: *An Spailpín Fánac* (qv), *Le Château* (qv).

See also: Cork Museum; University College Cork, Cork City Gaol.

BLUE HAVEN

3 Pearse Street, in the centre of Kinsale, Co Cork
Tel: 021 772209

Kinsale is a marvellous place with a fascinating history. It is often referred to as 'an English town' following the famous siege of 1601 when the Spanish held the town until a fateful battle on Christmas Eve when the English prevailed and the incident was said to have marked the end of Gaelic Ireland. There is a busy harbour, a lively town centre, delightful environs and some great hotels and pubs. And if Kinsale is the gem of Ireland's south coast then the *Blue Haven* is the gem of Kinsale. The place soaks up atmosphere and exudes quality. Its 18 bedrooms have recently been refurbished and the *Blue Haven* received the well deserved accolade of Egon Ronay Irish Hotel of the Year for 1986.

Its place as a pub is well established with fine bar food available all day in a room of character with a log fire. A partially covered and flower-decked patio is an alternative venue. There are good beers and wines also and the opportunity to indulge later comes from the well stocked wine shop which sells deli items from the *Blue Haven* kitchen. The restaurant - open in the evenings - is serious about fish as you might imagine. Incidentally the chef's name is Stanley Matthews and one wonders, bearing in mind the 'Englishness' of Kinsale, if he is named after the famous England international footballer. He might even have been born in Stoke on Trent!

Try also: *The Spaniard* (qv), *1601* (it's a pub!).

See also: St Multose church, the Old Head of Kinsale.

THE SPANIARD INN

Scilly, Kinsale, Co Cork
Tel: 021 772436

This is a fascinating pub with all the atmosphere you expect from
such a place but seldom find. The name is in honour of Don Juan del
Aquilla who led the Spanish troops alongside the Irish Catholic
forces during the siege of Kinsale in 1601. A sixteenth-century
Spanish nobleman adorns the sign. The pub has commanding views
over Kinsale harbour which can be enjoyed while sampling the
delights of the pub's cellar and kitchen on balmy, sunny days. The
Spaniard's stone-faced facade is decked with flower baskets through
the summer and its external attractions are well matched by the
delights of its interior. Low beamed ceilings, stone-flagged floors
and a wealth of local memorabilia including a gigantic salmon
caught eighty years ago off the Cork coast. At one time there were
several claimants to being its catcher! The food is straightforward
and reasonably priced and the stout deserves a mention being
creamy and satisfying. Three bars provide a suitable atmosphere for
all tastes with log fires in winter. Pat and Mary O'Toole, who own
The Spaniard, are presently improving its standards without
detracting from its essential personality. One outstanding feature of
The Spaniard is the catholic taste in music; here you can listen to
jazz, blues, mild rock (if such a term exists) and, of course, traditional Irish. The 'little people' are said to enter and leave the pub by
a tiny door behind the bar.

Try also: *The Man Friday* restaurant, the *Bulman Bar*.

See also: Charles Fort.

T J NEWMAN'S

On the main street of Schull, Co Cork
Tel: 028 28305

If personality makes a pub then it certainly did not miss out here. The delightful Kitty Newman presides over the pub with a great deal of style as did, I am told, her father Thomas J Newman who bought it in 1914 and whose name still honours the facade and her brother Tommy who took over in 1958. Tommy died in 1988 and Kathleen (Kitty) now controls both the pub and the off licence shop next door. It is a tiny one room pub, completely unspoilt except that at one time it had, surprisingly, a four person snug behind the window. Kitty will reminisce to her heart's content if you are prepared to listen about how they used to bottle their own Guinness and how the pub up the road only changed its washing up water once a year. The locals, she said, brought their own tankards but they still went into the tub! Newman's has attracted the attentions of the world media with recent entries in *Cara* and *Auto Bild*.

Schull, which is a great place for sea sports, stands on the northern side of the wonderfully named Roaringwater Bay facing the Calf Islands. 'The Isle of Wight has Cowes Week,' says Kitty. 'We have Calves Week'. And when the pub is closed a notice on the bar door says: 'Gone hang gliding - back with the wind.'

Try also: *Bunratty Inn* at the other end of the village; *Paddy Bourke's* on Cape Clear Island (boats from Baltimore).

See also: Crookhaven and Mizen Head.

DINTY COLLINS

In the village of Union Hall just off the N71 road between Clonakilty and Skibbereen, Co Cork

The charming village of Union Hall is in a wonderful setting across Glandore harbour. Jonathan Swift the writer, satirist and Dean of St Patrick's cathedral in Dublin lived here for a while in 1723 when he was writing *Gulliver's Travels* and gave it some recognition. More recently the village was the setting for David Putnam's film *The Battle of the Buttons* in which local people including many children took part.

Dinty's, as the pub is known locally, stands at the heart of the village and is one of five which all offer a variety of food and drink to both visitors and locals alike - and locals can come from as far as ten miles away. It is a well established pub probably dating from the last century and it has been tastefully renovated with a good tiled floor. There are two 'church pew' type alcoves offering privacy, and a wider drinking area around the bar. The menu is simple with a selection of home-made soups and sandwiches and bed and breakfast is available.

Try also: All the other pubs in the village.

See also: Kilfinnan Castle, Creagh Gardens.

AHERNE'S

163 North Main Street, Youghal, Co Cork
Tel: 024 92424

Talk of seafood in Ireland and the name *Aherne's* usually crops up.
It is in the pleasant resort of Youghal (pronounced 'yawl') on the
N25 trunk road between Waterford and Cork City. There is an
excellent beach and it commands a delightful situation at the mouth
of the River Blackwater. *Aherne's* is in the centre of town and is run
with a good deal of style by the third generation of the Fitzgibbon
family. There are two bars - both wood-panelled - and the famous
restaurant. Meals are available all day in the bars and at lunchtimes
and in the evenings in the restaurant. It recently took an Egon Ronay
award for Seafood Dish of the Year and the choice available is
abundant; the owners list lobster, prawns, turbot, sole, salmon (wild
of course), crab, mussels and clams. There is a good, reasonably
priced, wine list and a fine pint of stout. There is light classical
music on the piano on most evenings. Sir Walter Raleigh was once
Mayor of Youghal and there are claims that the first potatoes in
Ireland were grown at his home at Myrtle Grove.

Try also: *Summerfield's* and *The Anchor.*

See also: Myrtle Grove, Ardmore Round Tower, and the Jameson
Whiskey Heritage Centre at Midleton (qv).

SWEENY'S WHITE HORSE BAR

On the main road through Ballyshannon, Co Donegal
Tel: 072 51452

Ballyshannon and its near neighbour Bundoran form the gateway to Donegal, Ireland's most northerly county. The town is situated on the banks of the River Erne just as it flows into Donegal Bay and upstream a mile or so away is the huge artificial lake formed when the Erne hydroelectric plant was built. This modern edifice contrasts with the amazing amount of history that Ballyshannon has to offer with memories of Saint Patrick and of the first colonisation of Ireland 3,500 years ago - and don't blame the English! In the middle of town is *Sweeny's* an excellent family run pub which offers something for everyone. The bar is bustling with good stout and reasonably priced snacks are served there. The lounge is comfortable and has an open fire. At weekends the Cellar Bar opens and is an excellent venue for music mainly provided by local musicians. It is stone-lined, cosy and sports another open fire. Old photographs of the pub show boats moored alongside it before the river was diverted for the hydroelectric scheme. Today the horses of the local hunt are the more likely visitors.

See also: Assaroe falls and ruined abbey, Lough Erne, Beleek (for its pottery).

ARNOLD'S HOTEL

In the centre of Dunfanaghy, Co Donegal
Tel: 074 36208

The north coast of Donegal has much to offer and *Arnold's Hotel* in Dunfanaghy is an ideal place from which to explore its many treasures. The Arnold family have run this 36-bed hotel since it was established in 1922. It is perfect for families with a games room, tennis court and a baby-sitting service. It is also the village local and the Whiskey Fly Bar is very attractive and characterful with a good reputation for its Guinness stout and for a fine range of whiskeys and whiskies. The hotel bar, which is open to all, is also very comfortable and popular and the last time I was in there I bumped into Paddy Maloney of the Chieftains. I understand a good number of famous folk use *Arnold's* for a quiet break. The food served at *Arnold's* in both the restaurant and the bars can best be described as 'no frills' - just good value.

See also: Horn Head with its 600 feet high cliffs, Tory Island, Ards Forest Park.

CONWAY'S BAR

In the centre of the village of Ramelton, Co Donegal
Tel: 074 51297

What a wonderful old pub this is. To start with it is thatched, which is an attraction in itself, whitewashed and, in summer, flower-decked. Inside it is full of antiques, particularly memorabilia of the brewing and whiskey trade. Or should it be whisky? Most of the excellently preserved old mirrors here spell it in the 'Scotch' manner. But most of these long-gone distilleries were in Belfast with its strong Scottish connections. But they are beautiful: coming from Dunville's, Cowan's, Watt's, Henry Thomson and Co, and others, they form a unique collection. And they fit in so well in the wonderful dark stained wood of the walls and bars, the stools and high-backed chairs and the general ambience of several decades ago. Whiskey (and whisky) drinkers are well catered for with a wide range of both Irish and Scotch brands to choose from. The pint of stout here also has many adherents. Ramelton is perfectly situated to explore the headlands of the north Donegal coast and the delights of Lough Swilly including its angling.

See also: Lough Swilly, Fanad Head.

ABBEY TAVERN

On the hill leading from the harbour in Howth, Co Dublin
Tel: 01 839 0307

The first thing you see from the deck of a Holyhead ferry when Ireland comes in sight is the Hill of Howth. Its lighthouse, with its powerful foghorn, may be the first thing you hear, for its stands at the entrance to Dublin harbour. Before the years of universal commercial air travel Howth offered a welcome to all Irish folk returning home from the flesh pots and employment prospects of England. The town itself is a thriving holiday and yachting centre and the base for a large fishing fleet. Don't call it a suburb of Dublin for that is another town ten miles away. What you can say is that the better heeled commute from here to the nation's capital either by car or by the DART - Dublin Area Rapid Transit - for which Howth is the northern end of the line. It's an attractive place with the island known as Ireland's Eye just off the harbour where yachts and fishing smacks coexist happily.

The Abbey Tavern is popular with both residents and visitors alike. They respect its friendly atmosphere and cosy cheerfulness. The character of the place comes from a careful attention to detail and a refusal to accept brash improvements. The floors are stone flagged and much of the seating was previously church pews. The two downstairs rooms have open fires and the long front bar gives a taste of what you might imagine your grandparents would have enjoyed as their local hostelry. Music is important here and upstairs there are Irish evenings with dinner and entertainment. After dinner walk up the hill where at one time Dublin Corporation tramcars ran and look out for the pilgrims returning from England.

Try also: *King Sitric* restaurant.

See also: The ruins of Howth Abbey, Howth Castle gardens, the harbour.

BRAZEN HEAD

Lower Bridge Street, Dublin
Tel: 01 679 5186

Walk westwards along the south quays and after passing the Four Courts on the opposite side of the river turn left into Bridge Street and there down a cobbled alley is Dublin's oldest pub. No one knows its real age or even when the present building dates from. But there are claims that there was a tavern here in the twelfth century. It stood, I am told, at the bridge of the hurdle. Hurdle in Gaelic is *cliath* and the Gaelic name for Dublin is *Baile Atha Cliath* - the town of the hurdle ford. QED. It obtained a licence from Charles I in 1666 and was probably rebuilt about 1700. It has etched its place in history ever since.

Politicians by the dozen have supped and dined here. Robert Emmett lived here for a while and his desk is preserved as one of the many interesting artefacts the *Brazen Head* has to show. It looks historical both from the outside and in its myriad of rooms and passages; low beamed, smoky, dim, yet inviting and full of atmosphere. Unspoilt it is said to be and so it is - the more recent alterations have been stylish and within the character of the pub. The pint is well cared for and the food is bountiful with a carvery in the bar at lunchtimes. The restaurant is open for lunches and dinners. There is a separate music room with traditional music on most nights and either jazz or blues on the rest.

Try also: *Ryan's* of Parkgate Street (qv), *The Porter House* (qv), World of Guinness Exhibition.

See also: Phoenix Park, the Four Courts, Halfpenny Bridge.

DAVY BYRNE'S

21 Duke Street, just off Grafton Street, Dublin 2
Tel: 01 677 5217

Many people know of Davy Byrne's by its appearance in James
Joyce's *Ulysses*. The book doesn't tell us much about the pub
beyond the famous enigmatic line: 'He (Leopold Bloom, the hero)
entered Davy Byrne's. Moral pub.' Later there is a more precise
description in Bloom's thoughts: 'Nice quiet bar. Nice piece of wood
in that counter. Nicely planed. Like the way it curves.' The eponymous landlord himself appears and states his opposition to gam-
bling. Maybe that is why his pub is moral. J P Donleavy, another
literary son of Dublin, although once removed, takes a contemporary
view and maintains it is what we imagine a Victorian pub to be like.
The best way to learn about it is to visit yourself.

Davy Byrne's is slap bang in the heart of Dublin, just off fashionable
Grafton Street with its elegant shops, and close to Trinity College
and St Stephen's Green. Whatever its history it takes its place as one
of Dublin's best pubs with three comfortable rooms catering for
differing tastes. Its reputation for good food persists and it has
always been experimental in its drinks policy. When Dublin toyed
with cask beers in the early 1980s it was the first to install
handpumps. Australian, Chilean and Californian wines now add to
the established and conservative original range. And there is a choice
of good stouts. Who am I to disagree with Donleavy but I reckon
Davy Byrne's is more like what we imagine a 1920s pub to be like. I
particularly enjoyed the Cecil Salkeld murals and he was certainly of
that period.

Try also: *Bewley's Coffee Shop, Gotham Café* for posh pizzas.

See also: *Brown Thomas* and *Switzer* departmental stores in Grafton
Street, Trinity College and the Book of Kells.

DOHENY AND NESBIT

5 Lower Baggot Street, Dublin 2
Tel: 01 676 2945

This mid-Victorian building carries its age well and both the frontage and the interior give the impression of careful ownership. Nothing much changes here and there is an air of solid comfort. This is the politicians' pub standing as it does no more than a soap box orator's shout from the Irish Parliament - *Dail Eireann*. They gather in the early evenings and during parliamentary sessions this pub can be really busy. For not only are the politicos there but journalists, lawyers and, that modern phenomenon, the spin doctors as well. But it is a good place to search out famous Irish faces. During the day life at *Doheny and Nesbit's* is much easier. Better to see the marble-topped tables, wooden screens, old whiskey mirrors and all the paraphernalia of a well-run pub. There are two rooms and, unlike many of its neighbours, it concentrates on drink. It is usefully situated as a dropping off point for matches at Lansdowne Road, home of the Irish rugby union team.

Try also: *Toner's Pub* (qv), *O'Donohue's* (qv), *The Pembroke*.

See also: Merrion Square (Georgian houses), St Stephen's Green, the National Gallery.

JOHN KAVANAGH'S (THE GRAVEDIGGERS)

Prospect Square, off Finglas Road in Glasnevin, North Dublin
Tel: a public phone for outgoing calls only

In a chapter of his classic novel *Ulysses* James Joyce described a funeral procession out to Glasnevin. On arrival there and after unloading the wreaths he gave us this gem: 'Coffin now. Got here before us, dead as he is.' It would have come close to *Kavanagh's* which is by the rear entrance to the cemetery more properly known as Prospect Cemetery. Nearby are Daniel O'Connell's monument and the graves of Parnell, Griffiths, Casement and many of Ireland's martyrs together with some literary luminaries including Brendan Behan. Find it if you can. It is probably best to take a taxi although buses pass close by on Finglass Road. The cemetery walls stand close to the pub and a hole in the wall is said to have been used to pass pints through to gravediggers working on the other side; hence the pub's alternative name.

Six generations of Kavanaghs have run this pub since it was established in 1833. There are really two pubs here and the contrast couldn't be greater. No.1 to the left is basic, full of character, still displaying signs of its former existence as a grocery. There are wooden walls and eye-level dividers with swing doors and in serried ranks lie spice boxes that once sold tea, coffee sugar and of course spices. A skittle alley remains that is sadly no longer in use although the locals play rings as skilfully as folk in other pubs play darts. No. 2, otherwise known as the select, is plush, comfortable and relatively modern. It is broken up into comfortable alcoves for privacy.

Eugene Kavanagh, the present incumbent, is a great marathon man. He had completed 142 by the summer of 1996 including several of the major ones: Boston, New York, London, Dublin and Berlin. His best time was 3 hours 1 second and though he feels he is past breaking the three hour mark he says he will carry on running until he stops enjoying it.

Try also: *The Brian Boru* (*Hedigan's*), *Mulligan's* of Stoneybatter.

See also: The Botanical Gardens and for Joyceans Eccles Street is less than one mile away.

LONG HALL

South Great George's Street, Dublin
Tel: 01 675 1590

This is an appropriate name for a pub said to have the longest bar in Dublin. It is certainly a notable one made of highly polished wood with an impressive inlaid brass belt and foot rail. Behind it the curates dispense a fine pint of stout. A large clock called a regulator displays what it claims is the 'correct time' which is unusual for a pub which normally likes to be slightly ahead of its customers. Another, not so elaborate, pedestal clock is in the back lounge. Mirrors, screens with good coloured glass and fine panelling abound and a wild assortment of chandeliers light up the rooms. The walls are full of prints showing everything from cartoons of politicians to caricatures of Gilbert and Sullivan characters. An archway leads to a large lounge and on it are the names of former owners of the business. G V Hoolihan, a Kerryman, has presided here since 1973 and in the 150 years of its life the *Long Hall* has had only four owners. *The Long Hall* stands on one of Dublin's busiest streets and is a welcome haven from the bustle outside.

Try also: *Stags Head* (qv), *Porter House* (qv).

See also: Dublin Castle, Christ Church and St Patrick's cathedrals.

MCDAID'S

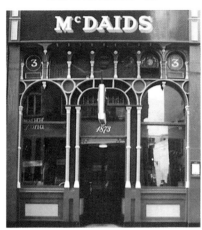

Harry Street, off Grafton Street, Dublin 2
Tel: 01 677 5272

This is a pub that has known its fair share of characters over the
years since 1873 when it was built and Dubliners still dine out on
the alleged antics of such literary luminaries as Brendan Behan,
Patrick Kavanagh and Brian O'Nolan (although the literary world
knew him as Myles na Gopaleen or Flann O'Brien). Behan is said to
have moved in for a while with his typewriter and taken over one
corner of the main bar. Noel Purcell the actor and Jimmy O'Dea the
comedian also held court here. Today it is the pub where they reckon
'that time stands still' and it takes its place amongst that classic
breed of literary and theatrical pubs in and around Grafton Street.
McDaid's is in good hands and quality remains as the main item on
its agenda. Hot lunches are highly praised and light, pre-theatre,
suppers are in demand. Pints are important here too and there is a
good range of spirits and wines. At one time it is said that during the
'holy hour' you could buy a take-out of a bottle of illegal poitín from
under the counter. The 'holy hour' is no more and neither is the
poitín! One thing you can look forward to at *McDaid's* is traditional
Irish music which is played most nights of the week.

Try also: *Davy Byrne's* (qv), *Cooke's Cafe.*

See also: Shopping in Grafton Street.

MULLIGAN'S OF POOLBEG STREET

8 Poolbeg Street, Dublin, 2
Tel: 01 677 5582

It is useful to know that this pub is always called *Mulligan's of Poolbeg Street* so as not to confuse it with other pubs called Mulligan's in different locations. They are, it might be said, lesser luminaries. It can be found between Trinity College and the Quays. Soaked in literary history, the pub has been here since 1782 and while changes have been made they have been discreet and it still retains its Joycean character. The attractive wooden front with its interesting windows draws you into an atmosphere of friendly conversation and good service. Much of its early days is remembered with dark polished wood screens, large Victorian mirrors, gas lighting, posters from the old Theatre Royal and a general ambience of a more gentle age. One claim made on its behalf is that it serves the best pint of Guinness in Dublin. The pub stands close to some of the city's newspaper offices and journalists, as I know well, have a sixth sense in sniffing out the best of drink. That many of them over the years use *Mulligan's* as their watering hole is reason enough to accept the claim. John F Kennedy drank here when he worked as a journalist in Dublin in 1945 and he is just one of the many famous folk who had and have a tender feel for the place. It is one of the best known and best loved pubs in Ireland.

Try also: *Horse and Tram* (Eden Quay).

See also: Trinity College and the Book of Kells.

O'DONOGHUE'S

Merrion Row, close to St Stephen's Green, Dublin
Tel: 01 676 2807

This is the home of traditional Irish music. It is where the Dubliners and many other famous musicians have gathered and played and is probably the best liked pub in Dublin. Miss it and you miss out on a cornerstone of Irish popular culture. It was built in 1789 as a grocery selling wines and spirits and it was not until 1934 that it became a pub. Its musical credentials date from the early 1960s when the Ronnie Drew Group, later to become The Dubliners started playing there. They were followed by such names as Seamus Ennis, Dominic Behan, The Fureys and Christy Moore. The present owner, Dessie Hynes took over in 1977 and the pub was largely rebuilt after a disastrous fire in November 1985.

The long narrow front bar has two entrances, only one of which is open at a time depending on how busy the pub is - you must visit the place to understand! The floors are covered in Liscannor flags and drawings of Dublin decorate the walls while high stools play sentry at the bar. The small back snug contains a massive collection of photographs of musicians from all over the world who have played there; Carnegie Hall and the Royal Albert Hall cannot compete. The scene is completed by a large covered yard with access to a food bar and the interest of many old enamel trade signs. And whatever reason brings visitors to *O'Donoghue's* it was the great pint of Guinness that won my vote.

Try also: *Toner's* (qv), *Doheny and Nesbit* (qv).

See also: St Stephen's Green, the National Museum, the National Library.

OLD STAND

37 Exchequer Street, just off College Green in the centre of Dublin
Tel: 01 677 7220

The Old Stand is owned by Dorans who also run *Davy Byrne's* which is no more than a dignified stagger away. It stands proudly on a busy corner, black painted with discreet gold lettering and pleasant window dressings. Like its partner, it is a stylish pub although of a lesser personality; darker, slightly more dignified and catering for locals rather than internationals. Not that visitors aren't welcome for this is a very friendly pub. Good value roast meat lunches at reasonable prices are in demand here and the pub has a reputation for steaks. The screened compartments along the wall are good places to dine in. There is also a smaller room at the back.

Try also: *Stag's Head*, *Good World* (the best Chinese restaurant in Dublin), *Bewley's*.

See also: Trinity College, the Bank of Ireland in College Green (once the Irish Parliament).

PORTER HOUSE

Parliament Street, close to Wellington Quay, Dublin
Tel: 01 702 4992

This is Dublin's newest pub, at least it was at the time of writing. It is also the city's newest brewery for within its capacious interior is a ten-barrel brewing plant from which a porter, two stouts, three lagers and two Irish ales are produced. It has been created in a derelict building and has three storeys or five levels depending which way you look at it. It is delightfully airy with a central well and is decked out in stripped pine. Look around and choose which part of the pub you want to drink or eat in. The restaurant on the first floor is quickly earning itself a fine reputation.

Appropriately, Plain Porter has quickly established itself as one of the favourite drinks at the *Porter House*. It takes its name from the one-time standard drink of the Dubliners although Porter was actually a London import. Flann O'Brien in his comic novel *At Swim Two Birds* eulogised the style:

> When money's tight and is hard to get
> And your horse has also ran,
> When all you have is heap of debt -
> A PINT OF PLAIN IS YOUR ONLY MAN.

Another beer, a strong Irish ale called An Brainblásta, is sold only by the glass. This play on words actually means 'a tasty drop.'

Try also: *Brazen Head* (qv), *Stags Head* (qv).

See also: City Hall, the Temple Bar district.

RYAN'S OF PARKGATE STREET

28 Parkgate Street, near to the eastern gate to Phoenix Park, Dublin 8
Tel: 01 677 6097

This is a splendid example of a high Victorian pub, what was often called a 'gin palace'. It was built a century ago to serve the needs of the newly affluent middle classes who would repair to it for up market drinks - spirits rather than beers - in up market company. It kept them away from the working classes in downtown Dublin. Today *Ryan's* - the '*of Parkgate Street*' bit identifies it from other less favoured *Ryans* in Dublin - is much more cosmopolitan. Its position on the north side of the River Liffey and close to Heuston railway station and the main entrance to Phoenix Park gives it special significance. It attracts locals, visitors, commuters, passers-by and the just plain curious. None are disappointed for the pub, which has been run for 75 years by members of the Ryan family, offers art, grace and aesthetics as well as satisfaction for the inner man. It has a magnificent carved oak and mahogany central bar with wooden stools which serves the main room and two cosy snugs. Screens and etched glass abound and a two faced mechanical clock does for both sides of the tall bar back. There are brass gas lamps and a superb collection of antique wall mirrors. Upstairs there is a 32-seater restaurant which shows off two period fireplaces. Ryan's recently moved out of family ownership but evidence suggests that no obvious changes will be made.

Try also: *Brazen Head* (qv), Irish Whiskey Corner, Guinness Hop Store and Brewery Visitor Centre.

See also: Phoenix Park, Kilmainham Gaol Museum.

STAGS HEAD

Dame Court, off Dame Street, Dublin
Tel: 01 677 9307

This is one of Dublin's great pubs, known across the world and a favourite of business people, tourists and what Flann O'Brien called 'the plain people of Dublin'. There has been a pub on the site since 1770 but the present one dates from 1895 when it was rebuilt in the high period of Victorian Dublin baroque with loads of mahogany and etched glass mirrors. The mirrors are magnificent, soaring to a lofty roof void and roaring out of them is a wonderful stag's head guarding the marble topped bar from which thousands of pints are poured each week. This is a busy pub. The main room is broken up by attractive screens and at the main entrance end of the bar large whiskey vats give it further appeal. Stained glass windows also contain the stag, a handsome brute that deserves the display he gets. Food is important here with simple but substantial fare at lunchtimes and early evenings. At the back is a comfortable snug with leather upholstery and the downstairs bar is the place for music.

Try also: *The Old Stand* (qv), *Porter House* (qv).

See also: The Temple Bar area, City Hall.

TONER'S PUB

139 Lower Baggot Street, Dublin 2
Tel: 01 676 3090

Toner's is the archetypal Dublin Victorian pub. Its predecessor
opened as a grocery and wine merchant on a nearby site in 1817 and
moved to where it is now about 20 years later. Some folk will claim
that 'nothing has changed'. The snug to the left of the entrance is a
delight with wooden settles and high stools to sit on and great pints
of stout to drink. This is the 'press' pub and in my experience
journalists only gravitate towards good drink and good value, so
follow their example. The main bar has high ceilings, dark stained
woodwork, gilded mirrors advertising long gone whiskeys and
enamel advertisements for cigarettes at five for twopence (old
money). A range of old drawers reminds us that a grocery was once
the other half of a pub's business. And while the handpumps are not
in use they add a touch of character and a hope for the future that
soon they may be back. It is a pub for conversation, although
musicians are catered for in the downstairs bar. William Butler
Yeats, the great mystic poet, is said to have visited *Toner's* - it was
the only pub in Dublin he ever entered. According to legend he was
not impressed; he drank a sherry and left. What a pity, he missed the
best part.

Try also: *O'Donoghue's*, (qv), *Doheny and Nesbit* (qv), *The
Pembroke*.

See also: St Stephen's Green, National Museum.

DONNELLY'S

Barna, Co Galway
Tel: 091 592487

Although it is no more than five miles from Galway's city centre Barna commands a personality of its own. This tiny seaside resort has a beach - the Silver Strand - that takes its place amongst the finest bathing areas in Ireland, and the village has other attractions including *Donnelly's* which is widely known for its seafood restaurant. The Donnelly family have run the pub for almost a century and their style is to let things take their own course. If change is needed then it takes place naturally; nothing flash, nothing pretentious, just aiming to retain good old fashioned comfort and friendliness. The restaurant in what was once the stables specialises in sea food and its position on the edge of Galway Bay makes this appropriate. In the bar other tastes are also provided for, steaks, chicken and the like. Traditional music sessions take place on Wednesdays through the year with more on weekends during the summer. For me its star attraction is the tree-shaded garden with its Liscannor slate furniture and pavement, and seasonal explosions of flowers. Here you can drink coffee in the morning, stout with the lunchtime sandwiches and wine with dinner in the evening. Perfect.

See also: Galway City, Salthill and Spiddal which is part of the Gaeltacht.

D'ARCY INN

Main Street, Clifden, Co Galway
Tel: 095 21146

Clifden contains a wealth of modern history. Remains of the first
Marconi transatlantic wireless station are here and close by is a
plaque marking the landing in 1919 of Alcock and Brown, the first
people to fly the Atlantic non stop. It is also a very attractively
situated town with a back-drop of the Connemara mountains and
magnificent views which repay the effort in short walks to climbs to
attain them. A tour of Connemara is a must for anyone visiting close
to the area which ranks as one of the most beautiful parts of Ireland.
And then, of course, there is the *d'arcy inn* with its street facing
narrow front and its long narrow interior, all turquoise and white and
full of interest. Modern yet classic in style. As one might imagine at
a pub in a town on the Atlantic seaboard the bar and restaurant
specialise in seafood. The particular favourite is lobster along with
crab and other crustaceans, but the menu is full of culinary fancies to
suit all tastes. The stout rates a mention and the wines are interesting
and reasonably priced.

Try also: *E J King's* pub, *Destry Rides Again* restaurant.

See also: Connemara National Park.

MURPHY'S

High Street, in the centre of Galway City
Tel: 091 64589

Murphy's Law is: 'if something can go wrong, it will go wrong'. But how wrong can such a law be for little ever seems to go wrong in this the most traditional of Galway pubs. To call it unspoilt is to undermine it for what few changes there have been since Philip Murphy bought it in 1931 have been for the better. It is basic, friendly, bustling and most welcoming. This one-bar pub is in the heart of Galway, Ireland's most exciting and genuine city. The road pattern dates back centuries and the houses match. All around are memories of the city's illustrious past and *Murphy's Bar* is part of them. At one time the pub sold groceries, a regular practice which now, sadly, appears to be vanishing particularly in urban areas but the lack of it does not detract from the atmosphere of this wonderful pub. Murphy's law is well displayed on the pub walls along with a number of other laws and dictums one of which is: 'celibacy is not hereditary.'

Try also: *Tigh Neachtain* (qv) and *The Quays* (qv).

See also: Lynch's Castle and the Spanish Arch and Galway races in July.

RABBITT'S

Forster Street, just off Eyre Square, Galway City
Tel: 091 566490

The centre of Galway remains as it must have been in the late nineteenth century with narrow lanes, high buildings and the lovely open Eyre Square at its centre. Just off the square at the railway station corner is *Rabbitt's,* a rather splendid classy pub which attracts the business folk of the city and visitors alike. A long bar on the left has high stools and facing this is a series of alcoves which give a degree of privacy to groups of customers. There is also a small off-licensed shop on the left of the door and well provisioned restaurant to the right. All three of the Irish stouts are sold here - Guinness, Beamish and Murphy's along with an interesting range of bottled beers: Grolsch from the Netherlands, Stella Artois from Belgium and Smithwick's Barley Wine from Ireland. There are also some excellent single malt Scotch whiskies and a full portfolio of Irish whiskeys. A piano indicates music and in season that means practically every night. In winter it comes somewhat less frequently. It is a friendly pub with excellent service as befits a business that has been in the same family since it was founded. Cormac Rabbitt opened the premises in 1872 after returning from a spell in California during the gold rush. Originally it was a grocery, then a bar was added, then a restaurant and more lately the off licence shop. Cormac's grandson and great grandson, Murtagh and John, are now in charge.

Try also: *Tigh Neachtain* (qv), *O'Connell's* (Eyre Square).

See also: The house of Nora Barnacle (James Joyce's wife) in Bowling Green and the old streets of the city.

THE QUAYS

Quay Street, in the centre of Galway City
Tel: 091 568347

If for any good reason the reader does not trust this guide then here is an opportunity to find out about this pub from a most unusual source. For *The Quays* is on the internet. Call up *http://www. commerce.ie/cf/fitzgerald* from anywhere in the world and you can find out what it has to offer. For those of you without such sophisticated facilities or being of a more trusting nature, then read on.

The Quays is a bit like a Tardis; a tiny facade hides an enormous interior. The small front bar is what is left of the original pub which dates from the seventeenth century and was called *Lydon's*. Three years ago the pub was extended and the lower levels and the rear of the pub are designed in a Spanish style reflecting the fact that for centuries there was extensive trade between Galway and Spain with the nearby Spanish Arch and other architectural features as memories of this. There are several bars in this area with others upstairs where there is also a flourishing restaurant.

The original bar which is popular with local drinkers holds one of the oldest licences in Ireland and it is easy to believe in its longevity. Music is a big feature of *The Quays* with sessions of traditional Irish, Jazz and Blues. The stage is a large pulpit which is backed by a pipe organ and many famous names have appeared here. This is a fascinating pub holding something of interest for most folk.

Try also: *Murphy's* (qv) in High Street and *Tigh Neachtain* (qv) in Cross Street

See also: Downtown Galway, University College library and the seaside resort of Salthill.

TIGH NEACHTAIN

Cross Street in the centre of Galway City
Tel: 091 66172

This fine unspoilt pub is more than a century old and was once the townhouse of Richard (Trigger) Martin, one-time Member of Parliament for Galway, legendary duellist and the man who founded the Society for the Prevention of Cruelty to Animals. King George IV, who gave the society its royal prefix nicknamed its founder 'Humanity Dick'. *Neachtain's* is in the heart of the city and beware, parking is impossible. The pub's interior is a hotch-potch of small rooms built as pews, cubicles and confessionals. There is a piano, though traditional music is the order of the day here. There are informal sessions on most evenings and folk musicians from all over the world head for *Neachtain's*. The pub has issued its own album recorded in the bar. The walls are covered with theatrical posters and there is a fascinating collection of 'tat' unequalled in any other Galway pub. The bar food is excellent here, reasonably priced and substantial, and there is a choice of stouts. A restaurant on the first floor is renowned for its seafood chowder.

Try also: *Rabbitt's* (qv), *Murphy's* (qv).

See also: The Aran islands (by sea or air).

GEAGHAN'S

Bridge Street (N18), close to the main square of Gort, Co Galway
Tel: 091 33065

A smart but unobtrusive pub on the town's main street which incidentally links three county towns: Galway (of course), Ennis and Limerick. A long bar on the right is full of interest with lots of Gaelic football and hurling memorabilia, and on the walls posters of great folk music nights both past and forthcoming. It is easy to get into conversation here with the first question often being: 'Where are you from?' Usually someone knows someone who knows someone who has been there, wherever it is. Talk of William Butler Yeats here is commonplace. He lived just up the road at Ballylee in a tower he restored for his wife. And across the Galway road he lodged during the summers with Lady Augusta Gregory and her many literary friends - Shaw, O'Casey, Masefield and the like - at Coole Park. The house has gone but the wonderful lake, park and woods remain, 'all in their mystic beauty' as Yeats might have put it. *Geaghan's* literary connections are less precise but it is the home of the town's poetry contest and a regular venue for good traditional music. The pint of Guinness is of prizewinning quality. In the Irish style the pub shares its premises with another business, in this case a video shop.

Try also: *Sullivan's Royal Hotel.*

See also: Thoor Ballylee, Coole Park (with visitor centre), Kilmacduagh cathedral and round tower.

ÓSTÁN INIS OÍRR

500 yards from the ferry stage on Inisheer, Aran Islands, Co Galway
Tel: 099 75020

The most accessible and smallest of the Aran Islands is Inisheer (Inis Oírr in Irish) which is just six miles from Doolin on the coast of County Clare. It takes only 30 minutes by the regular ferry service from Doolin and there are other services from Galway and Rossaveel and by air from Galway's airport at Inverin. The hotel is close to the ferry pier and most of the island's amenities. It is new in Aran terms dating from 1982 and it provides food, drink and accommodation. The main bar is airy and pleasantly light with lots of local and sporting photographs on the walls. Despite its closeness to Clare it is devotedly dedicated to County Galway particularly for sport. Locals pop in and out and speak Gaelic to each other but English to visitors - there is none of the insularity often found in the Welsh-speaking parts of Wales. The atmosphere is most friendly. A pint of Guinness costs less here than in any other part of Ireland; it's a strange irony that the further away from the brewery you get then the cheaper the pint becomes. It is all to do with the government's financial aid for the Gaeltacht areas. Music sessions here are spasmodic rather than regular but in the summer they are quite frequent. There is much to see on Inisheer, and indeed on the other two islands of Inishmaan and Inishmore, with archeology, flora and fauna to the fore. There is also a wonderfully clean bathing beach. Change is slow coming here and a visit is like travelling back fifty years in time.

Try also: *Tigh Ned* and *Tigh Ruairi* (pubs).

See also: Several ruined churches and castles and An Loch Mór a 16-acre lake that is wonderful for bird watching.

MORAN'S OYSTER COTTAGE

The Weir, Kilcolgan, Co Galway
Tel: 091 796113

This pub is a must for anyone travelling along the N18 trunk road that links Limerick and Galway. At Kilcolgan signs direct you to *Moran's* which is just half a mile along the north bank of the Kilcolgan River, an inlet of Galway Bay. It is all reminiscent of smugglers, shipwrecks and fishermen telling tall tales. In the last century this was a thriving port, now it is a great place for wild life and particularly sea birds. The pub is a genuine cottage, thatched and white washed with tiny tile-floored rooms served by a central bar with a cosy restaurant at the back and tables outside at the front. The Moran family have been here since 1760 and the present incumbent - Willie Moran - is of the sixth generation. He was the world oyster opening champion in 1989 when he notched up 30 oysters in one minute 31 seconds and he retained the title the following year. Naturally the star attraction here is a plate of oysters washed down by a pint of Guinness. Local oysters - Moran's have their own beds - are available from September to April and Pacific ones through the year. Crab, smoked salmon and prawns and occasionally lobster also figure on the menu. In Ireland stout always seems the obvious accompaniment to oysters but for those folk who prefer wine *Moran's* offer a good and reasonably priced selection.

Try also: *Raftery's Rest* (Kilcolgan) and *Paddy Burke's* (Clarinbridge).

See also: Drumacoo church.

THE OULD PLAID SHAWL

On the main road through Kinvara, Co Galway

Kinvara is a perfectly sited market and fishing village with the wonderful backdrop of Dunguaire Castle across the bay. In its day it was a great commercial port for transporting turf across from Connemara in the traditional Galway Bay hookers. It is renowned for this in song and story and each August Kinvara is the base for *Féile na mBád* - the festival of the sea. Hookers arrive here and take part in races to the Aran Islands in what is quite a riotous but well behaved weekend. There are curragh races too for those odd shaped canvas covered boats in which young men row their hearts out to be the best. The pubs of Kinvara do well out of all this. *The Ould Plaid Shawl* in particular because of its quality and atmosphere. And not just for one weekend; the pub is popular all the year round. It is a small pleasant bar, smartly attired and well serviced. The stout - both Guinness and Murphy's - is great and so is the *craic* - the chat - and the music. Food is available, not sophisticated but value for money. It's a top of its own league pub, doing very well what it sets out to do.

Try also: *Tully's*, *Linnane's Bar* (New Ross).

See also: Dunguaire Castle (medieval banquets).

SOUTH POLE INN

In the village of Annascaul, Co Kerry

Travelling towards the end of Europe's most westerly peninsula is quite exciting in its own right but the opportunity to learn about one of the world's great explorers comes some 25 miles short of that ultimate point in the village of Annascaul on the Dingle peninsula. Here is the *South Pole Inn* built and lived in by Thomas Crean, an explorer who went on three South Pole expeditions, two with Robert Falcon Scott and one with Ernest Shackleton. Crean was a native of Annascaul and when he retired from the Royal Navy he settled back there, married and built the pub. It stands next to the River Owenascaul in a delightful valley on the western edge of this pleasant village. It is relatively unspoilt, is still run by his descendants and retains many memories of its first owner.

Inside it is all wood: walls, bar, screens and furniture and its three bars are linked internally. All around are memories of Crean's Antarctic visits. There are photographs, drawings, newspaper cuttings and a locally-made model of Robert Falcon Scott's ship *The Discovery*. This is a welcoming, sun trap of a pub facing, appropriately, south.

Try also: The gaily decorated *Dan Foley's* (in the village) and *Dick Mack's* in Dingle (qv).

See also: Inch Strand, Minard Castle.

THE ANCHOR

4 Main Street, Cahirciveen, Co Kerry
Tel: 066 72049

Cahirciveen, or to be more precise nearby Carhan, was the birthplace of Daniel O'Connell the great liberator, the creator of Irish democracy. The family mansion is now in ruins but the O'Connell memorial church in Cahirciveen celebrating the centenary of his birth was built in 1875 after a planning dispute which involved the Pope. The village is on the Ring of Kerry a famous tourist trip that takes in the wonderful sights and scenery of the Iveragh peninsula. Here's a tip: travel anti-clockwise against the traffic for better views and a quieter run. You will then enter Cahirciveen on a most attractive run from Glenbeigh and Kells. It stands at the foot of the Bantee Mountain and overlooks Valentia Island from where the first telegraph cable across the Atlantic was laid in 1858. The Maguire family have run the village's favourite pub for many decades and in that undetermined period nothing has changed. It looks like a shop - which it is - with a pub name. The window is full of fishing gear which is sold inside along with pints and pints and pints. No better pint of stout will be found in County Kerry or anywhere else in Ireland for that matter. The counter-come-bar in the tiny front room serves the usual dual purpose and the overflow for drinkers is into the family's lounge. Here there are comfortable armchairs and an air of gentle domesticity. The locals drink here and with good reason too.

Try also: *The Point Bar*.

See also: Valentia Island and view the Skelligs.

DICK MACK'S

Green Lane, Dingle, Co Kerry
Tel: 066 51070

To talk of Dingle pubs is to talk of *Dick Mack's*. For in a town that is full of good pubs it is the one that everybody seems to know. The small fishing town that rules the Dingle peninsula is jam-packed in summer with tourists of all classes; back packers, coach parties, fishermen, cyclists, motorcyclists and folk in cars of all descriptions. They come for all sorts of reasons; many to see Funghi, Dingle's tame dolphin, others just to soak up the atmosphere and listen to the music. And, it seems to me, most of this motley crowd seem to gravitate to *Dick Mack's* at the same time as I do. It is another west coast pub that claims the adjective 'unspoilt' and it seems likely that no changes have been made in the reign of the MacDonnell family which started when Richard MacDonnell bought it in 1900. He was the original Dick Mack. The present incumbent, Oliver J, carries on the good work. He still sells leather goods and wellington boots and continues the shoe repair service his grandfather started around 60 years ago. Local scenes by local artists decorate the walls and are usually for sale. A tiny snug at the front was once where customers of the haberdashery paid their bills. Unostentatious to a degree, it serves and deserves well. Music is usually spontaneous and is often simply piano and voices.

Try also: *Small Bridge Bar*, the *Islandman* (bar and bookshop!), *James Flahive's*, *Tigh Mhaire de Barra* (for Dingle mutton pies).

See also: Dingle Bay and Funghi.

KRUGER'S BAR

Dunquin, Co Kerry
Tel: 066 56127

According to Brendan Behan, Kruger Kavanagh – from whom the pub takes its name – was 'the friend of many Hollywood film stars, various American gangsters, boxers, politicians and similar sporting personalities.' He is said to have dined with ministers and princes and there is an apocryphal tale that at one time there was a photograph in the bar of Kruger sandwiched between Presidents Kennedy and de Valera with a caption that read: 'Who are those two men with Kruger Kavanagh?' Whatever they say about the man he left a fine pub and his reputation was such that a plaque to his memory remains in the bar - 'In loving memory of Maurice 'Kruger' Kavanagh - scholar'. His successor Patrick O'Neill carries on his traditions. I had one of the best pints of Guinness I have ever drunk here and although the company and the weather might have affected my judgement it remains etched in the memory. *Kruger's* caters for all tastes and its many guises allow this: guesthouse, pub, bar or various Gaelic equivalents, it depends on what you read. The film *Ryan's Daughter* was made near here, a suitably wild spot for such a tempestuous film. This is Europe's most westerly pub and as the local saying goes: 'the next parish is Boston.' It was also the pub which on St Patrick's eve in 1971 the Campaign for Real Ale was formed. It started as a bit of a joke and became in the words of Michael Young who himself had founded the Consumers' Association: 'The most effective campaigning organisation in Europe.' The great pity is that there is no real ale.

Try also: *Long's Pub* (Ballyferriter) and *Cheers!* (Boston)!

See also: Slea Head and the Blasket Islands, the Gallarus Oratory.

COURTNEY'S

66 High Street in the centre of Killarney. Co Kerry
Tel: 064 32571

The present owner's grandparents bought this pub in 1903 for £470. Today Con and Bridie Courtney run it with style. It is the archetypal Kerry pub and probably the only one in Killarney to retain its original layout and design. Local drinkers predominate here but visitors are most welcome provided you leave your prejudices behind. The small front lounge has lots of interesting pictures and amusing notices. Behind the bar is a snug and nowhere is there canned music. This is a pub where conversation is not a lost art. There is a place for live music however and this is invariably traditional. Soup and sandwiches are available and Bridie specialises in Irish Coffee. The outside is painted in Kerry's colours of green and gold. 'It used to be blue,' said Con, 'but Kerry won the All-Ireland football in 1953 so I changed it then and we've stayed that way every since.'

Killarney is a splendid place for getting about from. The Ring of Kerry offers some of the most attractive scenery in Europe - nay the world.

Try also: *The Laurels* (qv) and *Dingle's* in New Street for fine food.

See also: The Ring of Kerry and the Magillicuddy's Reeks which include Ireland's highest mountain.

THE LAURELS

Main Street, Killarney, Co Kerry

The Laurels is an attractive enough name for a pub but the way it came about for this one is worth retelling. Thado O'Leary - the present owner's father - bought the pub in 1913. He owned a greyhound called Kilbrean Boy - there is a picture of it in the bar - that was entered for the 1930 English Laurels championship at Wimbledon Stadium in South London. The trainer had two other dogs in the race and didn't give the Irish dog a chance. But Thado thought otherwise and offered a cask of porter to his locals if it won. The other two dogs bumped into one another on the first bend and Kilbrean Boy ran on to be an easy winner. Telephones were rare in those days and calls from London took hours to connect. Thado arranged for the local chemist to take a call with the result but before it came through a local joker rang and said 'the dog has won' . By the time the real call came through the porter was finished. However, Thado bought the next door pub with his winnings, knocked the two together and changed the name to *The Laurels*.

This pub is in the centre of Killarney near to where the jarveys ply for hire with their horse drawn open carriages to drive you to the Muckross demesne and the lakes. It has origins in the eighteenth century and is really two pubs. At the front is a stylish bar, neat and smart, which serves great value food and a choice of good drinks including three stouts. It is a long room with an L-shaped bar, high stools, alcoves and open fires in winter. At the rear is one of the classic Killarney singing rooms. Irish folk music is the style and great fun is had by the many thousands that visit it each year. The entrance is in a boreen at the side of the pub.

Try also: *Courtney's* (qv), *YerMan's Pub* in Plunkett Street.

See also: Muckross demesne, Ross Castle, the Lakes.

AN SÍBÍN BAR

*In the village of Lauragh on the north side of the Healy Pass between
Glengarriff and Kenmare, Co Kerry*
Tel: 064 83106

This is a very old inn. Historical fact records that it was well
established before 1768 when 'Daniell Sullivane was innkeeper at
Laraght'. And in all that time there has only been one family in
control: first the Sullivans and later from the distaff side, the Smyths
with Richard Smyth the present licensee. It could be that when he
retires his daughter may take over and as she is Frances O'Sullivan
the original name will be restored.

Travelling north over the Healy Pass is a wonderfully scenic but
hair-raising experience and refreshment is imperative, so *An Síbín
Bar* is strategically sited as you reach the end of the descent. The
name is the Irish for a shebeen. In the past such unlicensed drinking
houses were often the base for the supply of illegal whiskey or
poitín. Today all is different and here is a most attractive and
welcoming bar. It has a main room and two smaller ones including
one for darts. Comfortable high stools sit at the bar. The front
windows are not as old as the pub but date back more than 200
years. Try an Irish coffee here for they do it well. On my last visit
they had just served a party from the Netherlands with eighteen of
them.

The locals here are big into Gaelic football - Kerry is one of the All-
Ireland greats - and there are many mementos on the walls. Across
the road is an amusing folly - an old petrol pump decked up in
Murphy's Stout livery. Do not attempt to fill up your car.

Try also: *MacCarthy's* in Castletownbeare, *The Purple Heather* in
Kenmare.

See also: The Healy Pass, Glengarriff and Garinish Island.

JOHN B KEANE'S

37 William Street, Listowel, Co Kerry

This is a small town centre pub owned and run by the town's most famous son: author, playwright and poet, John B Keane. One of his books is called *Letters of an Irish Publican*. It is a lively and warm place and whilst you might expect to find it full of visitors it is essentially a family pub, very popular with locals although there is certainly no unfriendly bar on strangers. Twice a week through the year there is pub theatre: on Tuesdays a one-man show called 'Estuary' and on Thursdays two players read *Letters to a Matchmaker*. Both are by John B as he is affectionately known. More recently an adaptation of his book *Letters from an Irish TD* has been performed. The stage is a small area that leads to the pub toilets - activity pub theatre! The shows are tremendously popular and visitors are advised to be early to obtain a seat. The pub walls are decorated with theatre bills, mainly of plays by John B in the great theatres of Dublin - the Abbey and the Gate. A three dimensional mural of *Sive* which is probably the most popular play performed by Irish amateur theatre groups provides a backdrop to the bar.

Try also: *The Horseshoe Bar* (qv) and *The Maid of Erin*.

See also: The River Feale for salmon fishing and Listowel Writers Week (July).

HORSESHOE BAR

10 Lower William Street, Listowel, Co Kerry
Tel: 068 21083

Flagged floors strewn with sawdust give the *Horseshoe Bar* an old traditional flavour for starters. And although it is smartly turned out it still gives memories of a bygone age and some of its souvenirs tell of this. A stuffed greyhound over the bar is just one example. In life it was Bearna Badghill and it won the Tipperary Cup in 1919. When the present owner's father bought the pub in 1940 it was there over the bar and there it remains. Two paintings of bar scenes by a talented American artist, Jay Killian, and some ancient theatre bills add more character to the pub. Kevin Woulfe who owns the pub is a chef and he prepares the bar meals and also dishes for the 25-seater restaurant on the first floor. The excellence of the food is matched by the quality of the stout and a small but superb wine list.

Traditional music sessions are held at the weekends and every day during the All Ireland *Fleadh Cheoil*, a great traditional music festival and competition. This comes regularly to Listowel during August and brings music sessions to every pub in the town and during the festival accommodation is almost impossible to obtain.

Try also: *John B Keane's* (qv) and the *Listowel Arms*.

See also: *Fleadh Cheoil* (August) and Listowel Races (September).

BAILY'S CORNER

Ashe Street, centre of Tralee, Co Kerry
Tel: 066 26230

Tralee is Kerry's principal town, busy, bustling and prosperous and always popular with visitors. It gets packed out during the International Rose of Tralee Festival at the beginning of September. Girls of Irish descent from all over the world are chosen to represent their country or region to take the coveted 'Rose' award. There have been a Swiss Rose, a New Zealand Rose, a Yorkshire Rose, several American Roses and many, many Irish Roses. The famous song from which the contest takes its title was written by a local musician. And during this period the pubs are busy as you might imagine; licensing hours, it seems, go out of the window.

Baily's Corner gets its share of the popular vote during Rose week and for the rest of the year. Its charismatic owner, Garry O'Donnell, sees to that. It is, he says, one of the county's social landmarks and who are we to argue with him. It must be one of the best looking pubs in Ireland and its floral decorations in season are a delight. The shop front style sets it off and picks it out of the ruck. Inside dark woods add character; there are high-backed settles and church pew seating, interesting artefacts and loads of atmosphere. Hot meals are served at lunch times and snacks and sandwiches all day. Garry is a chef and his food has won awards. The stout is great here and a full range of other drinks is available.

Try also: *Benner's Hotel.*

See also: Steam railway to Blennerville and its windmill.

JOHNSTOWN INN

Johnstown Village, near to Naas, Co Kildare
Tel: 045 97547

Johnstown is an ancient settlement and for centuries has been a stopping off point for travellers. Its name stems from its foundation in 1170 when it was named after the Order of Knights Hospitaller of St John. A predecessor of the inn would provide food and rest for pilgrims travelling to and from other religious houses. Later it was a coaching house on the routes into and out of Dublin - often a first or last stop at the convenient distance of 20 miles from the capital. Now it is an excellent place from which to explore the racing county of Kildare and the Wicklow mountains or even make a final halt before reaching the fleshpots of Dublin.

The Johnstown Inn has been tastefully restored to cater for the needs of the modern traveller and even has its own motor coach which takes visitors to such places as the Japanese Gardens and the National Stud at Kildare or to one of the several race courses in the area. Food is served all day here either in the lounge bar with its open fire or in the comfortable restaurant and in summer barbecues are held on the patio. Traditional music sessions are held regularly and live music also forms part of the craft fairs that are a feature of the *Johnstown Inn*. A wide range of crafts are on display including woodturning, potting, wrought iron work and bodhran making. There is no accommodation but the Sheridans who run the inn will make arrangements locally for you.

Try also: *Fletcher's* and *The Paddock* (Naas).

See also: Racing at Naas, The Curragh and Punchestown; Goffs for racehorse sales.

SILKEN THOMAS

The Square, Kildare Town, Co Kildare
Tel: 045 22232

'The complete pub' is what proprietor Joe Flanagan calls his emporium in the centre of Kildare on the main Dublin to Limerick and Cork road. It has five bars, a pub within a pub, a rooftop beer garden and a 16-bedroom guest house. The Flanagans have been here since 1975 and maintaining a standard of excellence has been their stated intention throughout. Silken Thomas was the tenth Earl of Kildare, known as such because of the richness of his attire. He was also known as 'The Sporting Earl', and the public bar carries this name. *Lil Flanagan's* is the pub within *Silken Thomas*; traditional with open turf fires and a regular venue for Irish folk music. The restaurant is open at lunchtimes and evenings every day of the week. A former hotel behind the main building is now Lord Edward's Guest House and one room is the bridal suite which is provided free of charge to couples who hold their wedding receptions at the pub.

Kildare is set in Ireland's race horse breeding and training country with the prestigious Irish National Stud in the town. It shares a site with the mystical and beautiful Japanese Gardens.

Try also: *The Barge Inn* at Robertstown (qv).

See also: Irish National Stud and Japanese Gardens, St Brigid's Cathedral.

THE MANLEY HOPKINS

Main Street, Monasterevan, Co Kildare

Monasterevan is a pleasant market town sitting squarely where the main Dublin road to Portlaoise crosses the River Barrow. Gerald Manley Hopkins, Jesuit priest and poet, spent much time here with his friends the Cassidy family in the five years up to his death in 1889 when he was Professor of Greek at University College Dublin. Nowadays he is remembered in the town by an international literary summer school at the end of June each year and by a rather classy pub. Hopkins's poetry was mainly of a religious nature but it was innovative and he made forays into nature. One poem, *Penmaen Pool*, about a visit to Wales contains this wonderful description of a glass of beer: 'ale like goldy foam that frocks an oar'. For that line alone it is appropriate that Monasterevan's smartest and friendliest pub should take his name. It has two rooms, different in style - one modern, one traditional - but both comfortable and offering good stout, food and service to their customers. At one time the town boasted a distillery, which closed in 1921, and a brewery which shut down four years later. The buildings remain. It was also the home of the renowned tenor Count John MacCormack. He lived at Moore Abbey which is now a convent.

Try also: *Mooney's.*

See also: Woodstock Castle and White's Castle (both in Athy).

THE BARGE INN

By the canalside, Robertstown, Co Kildare
Tel: 045 860453

There is something about canalside villages that draws folk of all
types to them. It may be the water, the boats, handsome bridges,
complicated locks, charming houses and buildings and pubs of
character that attracts them, or maybe a combination of some or all.
Robertstown has most of these engaging qualities; it certainly has a
pub of character. *The Barge Inn* makes most of its ideal position
opposite the pier where the Grand Canal reaches its summit between
Dublin and the Shannon. It has been modernised with a degree of
care that allows you to accept its ancient origins, for it probably
dates back to the building of the canal. A long bar serves several
drinking areas, not least the outdoor tables which are ideal for
summer evenings. *The Barge Inn* serves locals and visitors alike with
equal grace but it remembers its original purpose to cater for the
traffic of the canal. Commercial barges are no longer around but the
pleasure cruisers abound. Good food and drink are available for their
passengers after a happy welcome.

Robertstown is a good place to stop overnight for there is much here
to entertain the visitor. The former *Canal Hotel* has been renovated
as the home of a museum of canal life and the venue for banquets by
candlelight. Boat trips in ancient, but restored barges, are available
for the non-boat travellers. Mondello Park, Ireland's premier motor
racing track, is nearby. A few miles down the road are the twin
villages of Clane and Prosperous of which it is said that an ideal
marriage would be 'of a clane man and a prosperous woman'.

Try also: *The Cottage* in Prosperous.

See also: Peatland World, Lullymore; Robertstown Canal Festival
(mid-August).

THE MARBLE CITY BAR

66 High Street, Kilkenny, Co Kilkenny

The Marble City bar must be one of the most photographed in Ireland; it is certainly handsome enough to justify that claim. Kilkenny is the eponymous city named as such because of the black marble found in the area and celebrated in the song *Carrickfergus* although the significance of that Northern Ireland town is not clear:

> But in Kilkenny it is reported
> There's marble stones there as black as ink.

The busy High Street with shops, pubs, restaurants and what the estate agents call: 'constant passing interest' is the perfect place for such a haven of peace as *The Marble City Bar*. It dates from 1709 and was originally a merchant's house but it has held a licence for more than two hundred years. The present owner, Patrick Weir, renovated it with discretion and both the grand exterior and the splendours of the bar area with its genuine fittings and furniture are a testament to his good taste. The long bar with its graceful curve at the entrance end and its attendant stools is complemented by a set of a solid wooden benches. The lighting is subdued and the whole picture is set off by a magnificent etched mirror on the back wall. The stout is excellent, coming as it does from a proper cellar, and you are given a choice of Guinness or Murphy. Food is of a simple nature: sandwiches, snacks and the speciality of bockwurst in a baguette.

Try also: *Tynan's Bridge House Bar* (qv), *Langton's*, *Kilkenny Kitchen*.

See also: Kilkenny Castle, Jerpoint Abbey.

TYNAN'S BRIDGE HOUSE BAR

On Johns Bridge in the centre of Kilkenny City, Co Kilkenny
Tel: 056 61828

Entering Tynan's is like stepping back in time. On the right is a set of magnificent spice and dry goods drawers that were in use up to 40 years or so ago. For the front of this wonderful pub was a grocery up until then and the bar behind it was an ancillary. Today where the two cohabit it is usually the opposite way round with the grocery taking second place. During the Second World War, or what the neutral Irish called 'the disturbances', many of the dual purpose pubs gave up their grocery trade because of rationing. *Tynan's* carried it on until the 1950s. After admiring the boxes (each labelled with its former contents - cinnamon, ginger, ground rice and the like) and other tools of the grocer's trade, step through into the bar with its three-sided servery, tall, marble topped and highly polished. An impressive tapestry dominates the far wall and all around are lots of other interesting artefacts.

The Tynan family have run this splendid pub which faces on to the River Nore through three generations and the present licensee, Michael Tynan, has been here for more than half a century. Michael junior is around and is ready to fill the vacancy when his father hangs up his drinking boots. Kilkenny has established its place as one of the most beautiful towns in Ireland with loads of history and interest. A visit there will not go unrewarded and its ancient castle is a must.

Try also: *Marble City Bar* (qv), *Kyteler's Inn*.

See also: St Canice's Cathedral.

RISING SUN

Mainstreet, Mullinavat, Co Kilkenny
Tel: 051 898173

The Rising Sun is well positioned in the attractive village of
Mullinavat that straddles the main N9 road eight miles from
Waterford and 25 from Kilkenny . It is an excellent location from
which to explore the south-east of Ireland and there are ten letting
bedrooms with all facilities at the pub to enable you to do just that. It
is a great place for walking - the Clonassey water falls are nearby -
and golfers and fishermen will find plenty of scope for their
recreations.

The pub which is built of ancient stone and timber dates back to
1644 when it was an ale house. Nowadays it has an eclectic feel
about it whilst retaining its charm. It is a long building with evidence
of sympathetic restoration and extension. Inside one bar serves a
large room with an imposing fireplace. Several smaller rooms lead
off and there is also a large function room. Soups and sandwiches
are served at lunchtimes.

Try also: *Downe's* in Waterford (qv) and *Jack Meade's* at Ballycanavan (qv).

See also: Jerpoint Abbey, Clonassey Falls, Waterford City.

MORRISEY'S

On the west side at the southern end of Main Street in Abbeyleix, Co Laois
Tel: 0502 31233

On the main Dublin to Cork road as you leave Abbeyleix is one of
Ireland's classic pubs. But really *Morrisey's* is more than a pub - it
is an experience. Outside it is sombre yet resplendent, painted black
and gold; long, low and impressive. Inside it is as if you had gone
back fifty years or more. On the grocery side to the left large tins of
loose biscuits face enormous jars of sweets. Coffee and tea (their
own blend) are dispensed in paper screws. And hanging over the
counter, but sadly no longer in use is a delivery bicycle with its large
front carrier. Whilst making your grocery order you can have a cup
of tea or coffee and a sandwich and in winter warm your self by the
large iron stove. To the right is the bar from which the owner, Paddy
Mulhall, serves a fine pint of Guinness. Old advertisements adorn its
black wood walls along with serried ranks of bottles of spirits on the
shelves and ancient whiskey barrels are there for you to rest your
pint on. Paddy will also, if asked, tell you the history of his fine pub
which has been in his family for more than two centuries and allow
you to guess the purpose of a rather peculiar device that he keeps
behind the bar. (Be one up by telling him it is a cockroach trap!)
But being a bar and grocery is commonplace in Ireland; *Morrisey's*
is different. Paddy Mulhall is also an undertaker. And an auctioneer
and valuer. And a newsagent. And, as is the way in these things in
Ireland, probably also a poet. Ask him. This pub should not be
missed by anyone travelling within fifty miles of this small attractive
town.

Try also: *The Horseshoe Inn.*

See also: Timahoe Round Tower, Stradbally Steam Railway and
Museum.

VILLAGE INN

In the centre of the village of Coolrain just off the N7 to the west of Mountrath, Co Laois
Tel: 0502 35126

The Village Inn, also known as *Sheeran's* from the family that own it, is in the centre of Coolrain just a mile off the main Dublin to Limerick road, half way between the two cities. It is beautifully situated at the foot of the Slieve Bloom mountains and ideal for exploring one of Ireland's lesser known rural attractions. The Slieve Bloom Way for walkers and a well signposted route for cyclists and motorists make the area an ideal spot for a two to three day stopover. The travel writer Richard Hayward described the mountains:

'...they are both as sweet and delightful as their names and at any season of the year they fill the eye with beauty and the lungs with their fragrant delicious air.'

The Sheerans who own the pub also have a self-catering thatched cottage to let one hundred yards down the village street. The pub is thatched too and has open fires, locally-made wooden furniture and a general ambience of welcome and friendliness and a fine pint of Guinness. Set dancing, a wonderfully entertaining, complex and quite exhausting pastime, takes place regularly in the pub along with other traditional music sessions.

Try also: *White's* in Portlaoise (qv) and *Roundwood House*.

See also: The Slieve Bloom mountains.

WHITE'S

On the Main Street of Portlaoise, Co Laois

Eugene White's Select Lounge, to give it its full name, is a long narrow pub with two contrasting bars and with entrances on the town's busy main street and from the large car park at the rear. It has recently been renovated and extended and the new bar is light and airy with modern furniture whilst the older, established front bar has discrete alcoves as well as seating at the bar. This is a locals' pub but all are welcome and the atmosphere is cosy and friendly with just the right amount of bustle you would expect from a town centre pub and normally nothing louder than conversation. The exception is when the Irish soccer team is playing and then the television sound is turned up; otherwise the set plays to itself or is switched off.

This is a family-run pub with Eugene and his son Gerald behind the bar or acting as waiter and with occasional visits from Mrs White. Recently a small but interesting food menu has been introduced mainly aimed at the customers of the new bar. Such traditional favourites as Irish Stew and Beef in Stout are available at reasonable prices. You will find the quality of the Guinness stout here is unsurpassed and, to my mind, there seems little reason to drink anything else in this superb establishment. Portlaoise is a handsome county town with some fine shops and plenty going on including one of Ireland's premier jazz festivals in June each year.

Try also: *Egan's* (opposite), *The Welcome Inn*, *Treacy's* on the Heath.

See also: The Slieve Bloom mountains, the Rock of Dunamaise, Emo Court Gardens.

VICARSTOWN INN

In the centre of the village of Vicarstown, Co Laois
Tel: 0502 25189

Canal boats tie up in the harbour outside the *Vicarstown Inn* as they progress on that arm of the Grand Canal that stretches from Athy to Robertstown. Vicarstown is a picturesque village and the pub at its centre provides food, drink and accommodation. This is great fishing country with the River Barrow close by. The inn is 250 years old and the Crean family has been here for many of those running the pub and also a number of other businesses connected with the canal traffic. A pleasant unspoilt tap room greets the visitors entering from the road and at the back is a large modern lounge. The food here has a high reputation and reaches from simple sandwiches to more elaborate dishes with a full range of drinks available. There are six bedrooms at the pub for those who want to stay over a while, for this is an ideal centre to explore the Midland counties down to Kilkenny and up to Kildare. The pub can also arrange accommodation in two self-catering houses close by.

Try also: *The Anchor Inn, Daniel Dunne's Bar* (Stradbally).

See also: Stradbally Steam Railway and Museum.

STANFORD'S VILLAGE INN

In the village of Dromahair, Co Leitrim
Tel: 071 64140

Village Inn is the most appropriate tag for this splendid pub in Leitrim's land of lakes. It has everything a village inn should have: basic bars with open fires, a small restaurant and accommodation. Dromahair is a peaceful and pretty little village close to the southern banks of Lough Gill and in the middle of a superb area for walking, climbing and angling. West Leitrim is in Yeats Country that mystic 'land of heart's desire' of William Butler Yeats's childhood. Lough Gill was the location for his Lake Isle of Innisfree, where he proposed to 'live alone in a bee-loud glade'.

Dromahair stands on the River Bonet opposite the ruins of Creevelea Friary which dates from 1508 and was the last Franciscan friary to be built before the suppression of the monasteries. The McGowan family cannot count back that far but five generations of it have run this pub since Mr Stanford, the great grandfather of the present owner, opened it more than a century ago. And the front bar remains as it was on the day the pub opened, nothing has changed except a spot of paint here and a new method of dispenser for the stout there. It is the archetypal Irish bar. Music making is of a casual nature although instruments for itinerant musicians are available and on display including a well played family fiddle. Good straightforward bar meals are available all day and the restaurant is open at lunchtimes and in the evening for very reasonably priced table d'hôte meals. There are five letting bedrooms.

Try also: *Hargadon's* in Sligo Town (qv).

See also: Cleevelea Friary, Yeats Country.

DUNRAVEN ARMS

On the main road through the village of Adare, Co Limerick
Tel: 061 396633

The Dunraven Arms is an excellent hotel. It is more than 200 years old and fits well into what must be a contender for the prettiest village in Ireland with its broad main street, many thatched cottages, stone buildings and such a wonderful setting. Adare is a perfect stopping off place on the journey west from Dublin either for an overnight stay or just for a meal. The bar meals in the traditional bar of the *Dunraven Arms* are excellent and the attractions of the *Maigue Room* restaurant and the *Inn-Between Bistro* (which is across the main road) are very tempting. The price of food is remarkably reasonable and it is certainly a place to return to or even to divert for. The accommodation is first class with some imaginative touches and there are also self-catering cottages available.

Having established the internal qualities of the *Dunraven Arms* it has to be said that this is horse country and all things equestrian are available, particularly hunting, along with golf, walking and fishing. This is the Golden Vale where the lush pastures feed the dairy herds and the farms provide some of the best quality food in all Ireland. The River Maigue runs through Adare and the eighteenth century poets of the Maigue area are credited with the invention of the limerick. At a revival of the Poetry Court of the Coshma (meaning by the Maigue) a limerick contest was won by a venerable bishop who knew something of *poitín* or *uisce beatha*:

> The traditional poets of the Maigue
> Knew nothing of White Horse and Haig
> But *uisce beatha* hot
> Distilled in a pot
> Kept them merry, poetic and vague.

Try also: *Sean Collins's Bar*, *The Mustard Seed* restaurant.

See also: Trinitarian Abbey, Augustinian Priory, Foynes Flying Boat Museum.

O'KELLY'S PUB

In the centre of the village of Dromcollogher, Co Limerick
Tel: 063 83017

The story is told that Percy French, the famous song writer, tried to cash a cheque in the only bank in Dromcollogher (there are various ways of spelling it) and was refused. So he vented his spleen not just on the bank manager but on the whole town in a satirical ballad:

> Sez I, 'Have yez been to Drumcolliher?
> Ye haven't? Well now I declare,
> You must wait till you've been to Drumcolliher,
> And see the fine house we have there.
> There's only one house in Drumcolliher,
> For hardware and porter and tea,
> If your master would come we would treat him in Drum,
> Oh! Drum is the place for me.'

O'Kelly's is a wonderful warm and welcoming family run pub and whilst it may not have been the 'only house' referred to by French it serves the village well. The great song writer, who also penned such favourites as *Come Back Paddy Riley*, *The Mountains of Mourne* and *Phil the Fluter's Ball*, would have enjoyed it. It only opens in the evenings which is usual for many country pubs but the chances are a visit there will coincide with a traditional music session.

See also: National Dairy Co-operative Museum.

NANCY BLAKE'S

19 Upper Denmark Street, Limerick City
Tel: 061 416443

Nancy Blake's it is and *Nancy Blake's* I suspect it will always be although the eponymous Nancy is now called Mulcahy. This is one of the best loved pubs of Limerick. It is in the oldest part of the city and its past is all too obvious: a long narrow bar which is really a series of interconnecting rooms - snugs if you like. There are wood shavings on the floor, and except for the front bar the lighting is suitably dim to blend with the dark wood settles, stools and servery and there is a great atmosphere. Nancy runs a tight ship and this allows for a good deal of exuberance but no nonsense. Music is all important here and the many concert posters on the wall tell you this. It is mainly the responsibility of her son Donal who created *The Outback* which is out back - a newly built, partly open area with its own bar and the venue for most of the sessions. They are held every Sunday, Monday and Tuesday and other times as well. There are open fires, fine stout, well made sandwiches and all the qualities you could want from a good city centre pub.

Try also: *The Vintage Club* (qv), *The Locke Bar* (qv).

See also: Hunt Museum, Limerick Museum.

THE LOCKE

3 Georges Quay, Limerick City
Tel: 061 413773

The Locke is one of Limerick's most respected pubs. Respected not only because of the quality of its decor and service but because the owner is Richard Costello, a rugby union star who made the Ireland side several times and was a regular for Munster for many seasons. He gives the pub a touch of sporting life and it all helps towards the total character of the place. The location is important, with the Abbey River just before it reaches the mighty Shannon in its front garden with an attractive tree-lined walkway softly lit in the evenings. The Locke stands out with its imposing black and white facade and delightful display of seasonal flowers. The interior is wonderful, genuinely old and full of character. There are snob screens to separate areas, panelled walls, high backed settles and a general air of comfort. The food is eclectic and excellent with some good seafood dishes and puddings standing out. You can breakfast here from 9.30 am. The pub advertises itself as selling: Ales, Wines, Spirits, but it was the stout that attracted me and that is the usual criteria I adopt for initially determining entries for this guide. So be it, The Locke makes it quite easily.

Try also: *M J Finnegan's* (at Annacotty and also owned by the Costello family).

See also: St Mary's Cathedral, King John's Castle.

THE VINTAGE CLUB

Ellen Street, Limerick City
Tel: 061 410694

This is a real treasure that is well worth seeking out in the centre of this bustling city. *The Vintage Club* is a splendid 1930s recreation in polished wood and brass although it was established in 1822. A plush lounge opens off to the right of the entrance and this is Rumpole's Room. Without doubt John Mortimer's fictional barrister would be at home here with a glass of the house claret before returning home to 'she who must be obeyed'. The main bar stretches back to the depths of the pub with several alcoves with settle seating around tables and with high stools at the bar. There is a delightful raised and semi-private area at the far end which is also used by musicians who play here twice a week. This is a food-orientated pub particularly at lunchtimes where roasts, other hot dishes and a wide selection of sandwiches are on offer. There is an excellent wine list and I could not fault the stout. The decorative scheme is eclectic with many old signs and a general atmosphere of good living. *The Vintage Club* which is not a club but one of Limerick's favourite pubs, is clean and smart, smelling of polish and freshness; a delight to enter. Quin's off licence shop, which is part of the company, is next door and opens late every night. The pub is close to the shopping areas where two of Limerick's famed products can be bought: lace and cured hams.

Try also: *Nancy Blake's* (qv), *South's.*

See also: Arthur's Quay shopping centre.

ANCHOR BAR

Tholsel Street, in the centre of Carlingford, Co Louth
Tel: 042 73106

'Historic Carlingford' is perhaps an over-used phrase but there is certainly lots of interest in this fine medieval town where St Patrick is supposed to have landed on his return from Rome. There was a Norse settlement here and they used the place as a base for their pillaging and plundering. King John built one of his castles here to guard the harbour and there are many other fine buildings of varying periods. The town is scenic too, with Carlingford Lough and the Mourne mountains to the front and a backdrop of the Cooley mountains. *The Anchor Bar* in the centre of Carlingford is also O'Hare's family grocery and the two share a counter in the Irish tradition, and the bar is decorated with some fine old advertising mirrors. The O'Hare family have owned this business since 1860 and the present incumbent, P J O'Hare, is well known for the friendliness and quality of his service. A particular favourite here is oysters from the lough (£6 a dozen at the last count which seems remarkably good value). Other sea food is also on the menu along with home made soups and a good assortment of sandwiches. PJ advertises 'a great pint' and who am I to disagree. In the summer a pleasant sun trap of a yard with rustic seating awaits you.

Try also: *Jordan's Townhouse* (for food and accommodation).

See also: King John's castle, Taafe's castle, Holy Trinity Heritage Centre.

SAIL INN

In the village of Clogherhead, Co Louth
Tel: 041 22242

James Lawless, who with his wife Rosaleen runs the *Sail Inn,* has a
fine turn of phrase. When he wrote apologising for the delay in
sending me a photograph of his fine pub he said: '...summer is a
busy time for us and some things tend to get put on the long finger.'
It is with similar style that they run the *Sail Inn* which is one of the
last remaining thatched pubs in County Louth. The attraction of the
low slung whitewashed building fits well into this timelessness of the
village. Thatch is certainly not out of place here. Inside good bar
food is available in a cosy atmosphere along with good pints and
other drinks. A walk to the head itself is rewarding. It stands two
hundred feet above the Irish Sea and offers views across Dunany
Point to Dundalk Bay and the Mourne Mountains. It is also a good
place from which to explore some fascinating pieces of Ireland's
historical heritage.

Try also: *The Glyde Inn* (Annagassan).

See also: Monasterboice, Mellifont Abbey.

MCMANUS'S

17 Seatown, Dundalk, Co Louth
Tel: 042 31632

I was attracted to this pub by a news release from Guinness saying that it had won a gold medal for the quality of its stout - 'the perfect pint'. I checked it out and was not disappointed. The perfect pint is an absolute so the only qualification I will issue is that it would be on the short list and some of the others on that list have yet to be found. And what a place to drink it in: a handsome bar of highly polished wood with an amazing collection of enamel trade signs to decorate the walls. There are many more in the beer garden, mainly advertising long lost beers and tobacco products. But strategically situated by some splendid shrubs is one warning: 'Prevent Forest Fires'. The beer garden at *McManus's* is amazing. It is on the roof of the pub, broken up into several areas and during the summer is an absolute blaze of colour with flowers of every description. The pub is in the oldest part of town and has been in business for more than a century. Brendan and Lilian McElarney who are the present owners are continually seeking to improve facilities and have recently installed a traditional Irish kitchen. Their motto is 'Simply a good pub' and you can't fault it. Ask for a glass of The Tyrconnell single malt whiskey; it is made close by at Ireland's smallest and only independent distillery.

Try also: *The Windmill Tavern, The Central Bar.*

See also: The Windmill, Castletown Castle, Racing at Dundalk.

MORNING STAR

In the village of Tullyallen, two miles west of Drogheda, Co Louth
Tel: 041 37400

The Boyne valley is one of the most attractive areas of Ireland's
eastern coastal fringe and also very historic. The town of Drogheda,
then one of the most important in Ireland, resisted siege in 1641 but
it fell to Cromwell eight years later and 2,000 of its inhabitants were
slaughtered. The Battle of the Boyne took place in 1690 when
William III defeated his father-in-law James II whom he had deposed
during the previous year. It was around Tullyallen, in what is now
known as King William's Glen, that the Williamite forces gathered
before their approach. Nowadays all is peaceful and the pleasant and
conveniently sited village contains the oldest pub in County Louth -
The Morning Star. It is thatched and its origins lie around the time
of the Battle of the Boyne. Michael Flood and his family run this
attractive pub with its comfortable lounge and larger function room.
Good bar food is complemented by an excellent pint of Guinness.
These can be enjoyed outside on balmy days.

Try also: *Foley's*, *The Thatch*.

See also: Newgrange, Millmount Museum.

BYRNE'S

Main Street, Castlebar, Co Mayo
Tel: 094 21561

The capital town of Mayo is a great place from which to explore this most enjoyable part of Ireland. It is the crossroads of the county with plenty of attractions including the attractive tree lined Mall - not to be confused with that American horror the shopping mall. They go big on sport in Mayo with Gaelic Football and Hurling at the fore. And *Byrne's* is the pub to go to if you have sporting interests. Mick Byrne - 'the boss' they call him - is the third generation to of his family to run the pub and he is the Chairman of the Castlebar and Mitchels branch of the Gaelic Athletic Association. His involvement stretches further with sponsorship of the Mayo Sports Star awards. In the pub there are many other sporting connections including its own golf society, and not surprisingly, for Mick is something of a star at the game.

The front of the pub houses the main bar, long and elegant, with good quality fittings. Behind a screen is a more relaxed, squat room with a television set that seems permanently tuned to sports channels. Mirrors with etchings of various sporting characters adorn the walls. One character who adorned the bar for a short while was George Best the former Northern Ireland soccer international who was said to have had 'a great time'.

Byrne's is twinned with *Flanaghan's* in Navarro, Italy. This is a concept devised by Guinness to attach characterful pubs in Ireland with Irish theme pubs in several European countries. Visits between the customers of the pubs are anticipated and other connections are encouraged. The author wishes the idea well but his views on Irish theme pubs are well stated in the introduction to this book.

Try also: *Flannelly's* in Castlebar, *Matt Molloy's* in Westport (qv).

See also: The round tower at Turlough.

MELLETT'S

Market Street, Swinford, Co Mayo
Tel: 094 51122

A trip back in time is what you will get in this two centuries old bar in the centre of the congenial market town of Swinford. It opened in 1797 with a Mellett in charge and seven generations later nothing much has changed with a Mellett still at the helm. In its time the bar has shared its occupancy with a grocer, an undertaker, auctioneer, estate agent, and a travel agency; and the Melletts were also farmers. In the old days the shop was at the front and the bar was entered from a door down an alley. Even today the pub is flanked by a newsagency and a branch of a building society, both run by the Melletts. A plaque on the front wall lists the Christian names of all the landlords.

There is a fine long wooden bar with screens and a number of alcoves together with a stocky back room all offering a little privacy - perhaps for farmers doing their wheeling and dealing? The whole place is full of bric-a-brac with old trade cards, posters of long gone events and a, sadly, no longer in use set of ancient hand pumps. There are open fires too for the appropriate time of the year. Food of a simple nature is available at most times.

Try also: *Egan's* (known as *Rice's*), *Anglers Tavern.*

See also: Swinford Fair in August.

MATT MOLLOY'S

Bridge Street, Westport, Co Mayo
Tel: 098 26636

'Seven Day Licence' is what it says above the entrance door to *Matt Molloy's Bar* in Westport, a reminder of the days when many pubs closed on the Sabbath and only the fortunate ones opened every day. The town is beautifully situated at the head of Clew Bay and is a popular sea fishing centre. The pub dates back to 1896 when the McGing family - a well known name in Westport - owned it with Dan McGing holding the licence until Matt acquired it in 1989. It was one of the famous Irish grocery and bars where everything needed for the kitchen could be bought from bacon to the frying pan to cook it in. Matt preserves the memory by displaying many of the items that his predecessors sold there.

There are no video games, juke boxes, fruit machines or television sets in this pub but there is a surfeit of live music which is not unexpected as Matt is a member of Ireland's most famous band, The Chieftains, and pictures of it are on all the pub's walls. His instrument is the flute and when he is at home he often takes part in the organised and impromptu sessions that seem to be the essence of his pub. *Matt Molloy's Bar* is always busy whatever the time of day or year but it manages without any difficulty to ooze atmosphere and it is the sort of pub you want to be in. Matt and his wife Geraldine have kept the authentic touch for this superb pub and with it a degree of intimacy, warmth and friendliness. And as well as the music there is a fine pint of Guinness.

Try also: *The West Bar*, *John McGing's* and *Hoban's*.

See also: Westport House and Zoo gardens, Clew Bay and Croagh Patrick (Ireland's holy mountain).

THE COCK TAVERN

In the village of Gormanstown, Co Meath
Tel: 01 8413530

Welcome to the oldest pub in the land! That is the greeting you get
on an interesting and detailed history of *The Cock Tavern*, the village
of Gormanstown and its surroundings. Elsewhere comes a slightly
qualified statement from the present proprietor Robert McAuley
which says: '...reputed to be Ireland's oldest tavern'. Its origins are
unclear but a substantial claim is made for it becoming an inn in the
thirteenth century. And despite the presence of a cock on the sign
this pub is not so named because it was a venue for cock fighting as
most others of similar name are. It comes from the family of Cok or
Symcok who were landowners in the area, and nearby lies Cock Hill.
The inn was established before the road from Dublin to Drogheda
and Belfast was built but from then on took its place as one of the
principal staging posts for coaches running between Ireland's two
main cities. Cromwell is said to have stopped here on his way to
Drogheda with his 13,000 men. It was a refuge for Mick Collier,
Ireland's most famous highwayman, but it was here that he was
finally captured in 1807. It was then, and remains, a place of good
cheer with bar food all day and excellent Guinness and other drinks.
For two years it was Meath Pub of the Year. Music comes in large
doses, organised and impromptu. Buying the house a drink could
obtain eternal fame for you as it did for a humble carter who stopped

the early days of this century and for whom a local poet penned this verse:

> So I ordered beauteous Lena to get them all a gill
> And with some rare agility this maid began to fill
> I slapped out on the counter a ready new half-crown
> For which I was applauded in The Cock of Gormanstown.

I suspect a round there today would cost a deal more than a half-crown.

Try also: *The Cottage Inn* in Laytown.

See also: Gormanstown Castle; horse races on the beach at Bellewstown in July.

BOGGAN'S

In the village of Rathcore, Co Meath (take the Trim road from Enfield and turn left after one mile, signposted Rathcore)
Tel: 0405 41167

This is as good an example of a Irish rural pub as you will find in a long day's march. It is not easy to find but the welcome you receive makes the journey all worth while. The pub has been in the ownership of the same family for more than a century and the present incumbent is James Boggan who runs it with a good deal of character. It has a traditional bar and a comfortable lounge, nothing special by way of food - maybe a sandwich - and an excellent pint. Its external attractions are appealing with a perfect example of thatching, even over the side door. There is traditional music on Saturdays. This is a great area for fishing with the River Boyne and the Royal Canal both well stocked.

Try also: James *Griffin's Bar* in Trim (qv), *Flattery's* of Enfield, *John Shaw* in Summerhill.

See also: Trim castle, the Hill of Tara.

JAMES GRIFFIN'S BAR

High Street, Trim, Co Meath
Tel: 046 31295

This is the heartland of Irish civilisation. Close by Trim (which appropriately-named town once won the Irish Tidy Towns competition) are such places as the Hill of Tara, Newgrange (where the sun shines into the burial chamber on the shortest day of the year) and a church where Jonathan Swift was once the incumbent. Richard II imprisoned the two young princes in Trim Castle, and Cromwell massacred many of the inhabitants when he sacked the town in 1649. Trim Castle is the largest Anglo-Norman fortress in Ireland and parts of it date from the thirteenth century. The Wellesley family, of which the Duke of Wellington – soldier and politician – was a member, lived at Dangan castle near Trim and young Arthur went to a school in the High Street and no doubt passed the pub that is now called *James Griffin's Bar* and which stands within the shadow of the great castle. It is a popular, traditional pub with good drink and lots of character. The lounge to the right is comfortable and there is a smaller Select Bar which is an appropriately atmospheric name for the room. The proprietor is Michael Lenihan who will fill you in on the fascinating history of Trim and its surroundings.

Try also: *Brogan's* (also has accommodation), the *Dean Swift*.

See also: Trim Castle, the Yellow Steeple, St Mary's Abbey.

THE FOUR PROVINCES

*In the village of Rathallen, Co Roscommon, on the N61 road five miles
south of Boyle*

I suspect the pub is named after the four ancient, and modern,
provinces of Ireland –Ulster, Munster, Leinster and Connacht.
However despite being in the sticks, this pub attracts great crowds
particularly at the weekends and its car park, the size of two football
pitches, reflects this. It is a modern building although there has been
a pub on the site for many years. The front lounge bar is comfortable
with a general air of welcoming 'busyness'. The larger back room is
used mainly at weekends for live music sessions and when there is
dancing - one of the big attractions - in what is not quite a Ballroom
of Delight but coming close.

The tiny village of Rathallen hardly rates an entry on most maps but
it is well situated for the many delights of this inland county. Lough
Key with its Forest Park is just a few miles to the north. On an island
in the lake are the ruins of the Abbey of the Trinity which was
founded by the White Canons. Boyle town is also worth a visit and is
a good place to tour from. The great popular song writer, Percy
French was born a few miles south of here at Cloonyquin.

See also: Boyle Abbey, Lough Key Forest Park, Lough Gara.

HARGADON'S

O'Connell Street, in the heart of Sligo Town, Co Sligo
Tel: 071 70933

Talk to anyone who knows the Irish pub scene and sure enough the name of *Hargadon's* will jump very quickly into the conversation. It became a pub in 1868 when it was owned by Matt Collery a member of the Westminster parliament. His name can be found on the clay whiskey jugs on the shelves of the bar. The Hargadon family bought it in 1908 and the pub has been with them every since. And during that period little has changed. The *Financial Times* waxed surprisingly lyrical in 1990: 'A pub seemingly unaltered since the last century. Its interior is dark brown and sombre, a turf fire glows in one corner, old bottles lean on sagging shelves...' I can't disagree. Over the marble-topped bar are served pints by the dozen, the score, the thousand and the reputation of *Hargadon's* Guinness spreads far and wide. The scene was well established when the Abbey Theatre in Dublin used the bar as a model for its production of John B Keane's play *The Field*. There are stone floors, dark wood surrounds, four snugs, turf fires, a roaring metal stove, mirrors, brass ornaments, Guinness posters from the thirties and, it will come as no surprise, loads of atmosphere. The locals help create it but the visitors help maintain it. Accept therefore that there will be no piped music, no fruit machine and no television for this is a talking pub where the art of conversation is crafted to degree standards. Bar food, a recent innovation, is of a very high standard. There is also a small dining room and a beer garden.

In Sligo we are in Yeats Country although, as one critic put it, Yeats, almost a teetotaller, won't feature much in *Hargadon's*. It is, however, in his 'land of heart's desire' and close by are Lissadell House, where he spent much of his formative period, and Ben Bulben, the mountain under whose bare head the poet was eventually buried and where his own epitaph can be found:

> 'Cast a cold eye
> On life, on death
> Horseman, pass by!

Try also: *The Cruiskeen Lawn*, *Beezie's*, *Truffle's* restaurant.

See also: Sligo Abbey, Lissadell House, Drumcliff Churchyard (for the grave of Yeats).

KILLORAN'S

Teeling Street, Tubbercurry, Co Sligo
Tel: 071 85679

Killoran's, or to give it its full name: *Killoran's Travel Agency and Traditional Restaurant and Lounge*, is full of interest and activity. Enter through the travel agency where they will arrange your next night's stay for you or even a fortnight in Majorca and then enter the long bar which opens at nine in the morning for tea, coffee and Anne Killoran's magnificent scones. Stay a while and enjoy a pint or two of Tommie Killoran's well-kept stout. Or a meal. Or an evening's entertainment. Variety is the key word in this most eclectic of pubs. It is full of antiques including a gigantic stew pot used in Famine times. Thursdays in summer are the best nights to visit with meals of sturdy Irish favourites such as boxty, crubeens (pigs feet) and champ to the accompaniment of traditional Irish music and dancing. You can even try your hand at butter churning. The everyday menu includes salmon caught in the River Moy a few yards from the pub's back door.

Anne was Sligo Person of the Year in 1993 in recognition of the work she does for many charities, particularly for the Down's Syndrome Association of Ireland. Her many awards for good works, including one from the Rose Fitzgerald Kennedy Trust in the United States, decorate the rooms of the pub. The Killoran family have run the pub which is the oldest house in the town since 1958 and when they moved in they paid a weekly rent of two pounds. Tubbercurry is a pleasant little town in an area good for fishing.

Try also: *Hargadon's* in Sligo Town (qv) and *Mellett's* in Swinford (qv).

See also: Banada Abbey.

DOWLING'S

At the south end of Main Street, Cashel, Co Tipperary
Tel: 062 62130

Dowling's is also confusingly known as *Meaney's* after a previous owner but either name will secure directions to this delightful little pub. It is wonderfully atmospheric, dark with red painted wood screens and an oak bar counter. To the right is a small lounge with lots of photographs of the town in former days and many sporting pictures. Behind the street window is a tiny snug with a sliding screen that ensures privacy from the rest of the bar for the three people that can squeeze into it. This is a great music venue with regular sessions at the weekends and occasional ones as they erupt. They serve generous sandwiches and good stout.

Arthur Guinness's father worked in the town as steward to the Archbishop of Cashel and lived in what is now the *Cashel Palace Hotel*, but that was before the days of Irish stout. The Rock of Cashel - St Patrick's Rock - which dominates the town is said to be 'the noblest cluster of medieval monuments in Ireland'.

Try also: *Cashel Palace Hotel, Chez Hans, Glasheen's* (Holycross).

See also: The Rock of Cashel, Holycross Abbey, Longfield House.

JACK MEADE'S

Just under the bridge on the Cheekpoint road from Waterford, Co Waterford
Tel: 051 73187

The Hartley family have run this pub for more than 150 years although it has been in business since 1703. This most attractive of pubs keeps its personality well and reeks of atmosphere. The main bar with its open fireplace is to the left of the door with two alcoves offering some privacy. Across from it is the Tap Room which is more open and ideal for larger groups. There is lots of bric-a-brac with ancient maps of the area and a price list from 1953 showing Guinness Porter at one shilling for a pint and Stout at one shilling and threepence. That's old money of course.

Food is of a simple but adequate nature including some well-filled sandwiches. During the summer there is a barbecue in the extensive garden and there is a roof top drinking area at the rear of the pub. Also in the grounds is a museum of agricultural life, a limekiln, an icehouse for preserving fish and access to some splendid river walks and good bird watching. Families are most welcome at *Jack Meade's* which is in a most delightful corner of Ireland with wonderful views of Waterford harbour from Cheekpoint and Passage East just a few miles away.

Try also: *McAlpin's Suir Inn* at Cheekpoint, *Downe's Pub* in Waterford (qv).

See also: The view from Cheekpoint Hill, historic Waterford City.

DOWNES'S PUB

8 Thomas Street, Waterford, Co Waterford
Tel: 051 74118

This wonderful pub was founded in 1797 by Henry Downes, bachelor and only brother in the Downes family so the line and ownership of the pub was continued after his death on the distaff side by the de Bromheads, but the firm remains Henry Downes and Company. The first business was that of a tea, wine and spirit merchant and at one time twelve different whiskeys were blended. Now only one remains but it is a classic. 'Number Nine' is a twelve-years old blend and is much sought after. When there was a choice and customers asked for 'the best' they were served with Number Nine. Another story says that it was the spirit favoured by the parish priest. Both tales are probably true. The outside of the pub according to one of the directors, Johnny de Bromhead, 'is rather dull'. But the inside, in my words, is something special. In one bar there are wood lined walls and settles and a tiny hatch servery. The other is larger with screens, wood panelling, a more open bar and a fine collection of pictures, advertisements and mirrors. The furniture is all good quality heavy wood and a high degree of comfort and service is assured. Above all try the Number Nine Whiskey.

Waterford is an important town and port and there is much to offer the visitor. Of particular interest is the Waterford Glass factory - the largest crystal factory in the world. Pleasant seaside resorts such as Tramore and Dungarvan on the nearby coast are well worth seeking out.

Try also: *Jordan's*, *Jack Meade's* at Ballycanavan (qv).

See also: Waterford Glass factory, Reginald's Tower, the two cathedrals.

SEAN'S BAR

Main Street, Athlone, Co Westmeath
Tel: 0902 92358

This is yet another pub that claims to be the oldest in Ireland. A brochure says it was established in 1630 and there is a list of owners, but whether it was run as an inn from then is not certain. It was called *The Three Blackamoors Heads* from the late seventeenth century which is a more likely time. The 1630 date is I suspect a piece of wistful thinking. In any case I believe there are other and better documented claimants to the title: *The Cock* at Gormanstown in Co Meath (qv) and *The Brazen Head* in Dublin City (qv). However of two things there are no doubt: this is a very old pub and it is a fine pub. It has entrances on to the improbably named Main Street which is only about fifty yards long and quite narrow and to the River Shannon tow path at the back. The front is classical although the four Ionic pillars came from a Dublin store and the yard and beer garden behind are quite modern. The interior is long, narrow, atmospheric, smokey, low ceilinged and very comfortable. There are high backed wooden settles and solid furniture. My use of the word 'atmospheric' although chosen some time ago was vindicated when *Sean's* was presented recently with an Egon Ronay award for atmosphere. Food doesn't stretch much beyond a sandwich but they are cheap and excellently made. According to Sean Fitzsimons who owns the place: 'we have music most nights of the year' and I don't suppose many pubs can say that. The River Shannon which backs on to *Sean's Bar* is important to Athlone and there is an inland harbour from which angling, boating and cruising are all available.

Try also: *The Mill Bar, Restaurant Le Chateau.*

See also: Athlone Castle, River Festival (June/July).

THREE JOLLY PIGEONS

On the N55 in the village of Lissoy, Co Westmeath

This is Oliver Goldsmith country. The author of *She Stoops to Conquer* was born hereabouts, and although there is uncertainty about where and when we do know he lived and went to school in Lissoy which became 'sweet Auburn' in his great poem *The Deserted Village.* He describes the village inn:

> Near yonder thorn, that lifts its head on high,
> Where once the sign-post caught the passing eye,
> Low lies that house where nut-brown draughts inspired,
> Where grey-beard mirth and smiling toil retired,
> Where village statesmen talked with looks profound,
> And news much older than their ale went round.

And in *She Stoops to Conquer* Toby Lumpkin sings the pub's praises:

> Let some cry up woodcock or hare,
> Your bustards, your ducks, and your widgeons;
> But of all the birds in the air,
> Here's a health to the Three Jolly Pigeons.

The present pub may be nothing like the one of Goldsmith's poem, probably dating from the late eighteenth or early nineteenth century whereas the poem was written in 1770. It has an ancient feel about it with part of the roof in thatch and the furniture and decor having that comfortable, well-lived in appeal. Locals are good talkers around here and conversation is not a lost art in the *Three Jolly Pigeons*. It may have something to do with the quality of the stout.

Try also: *Sean's Bar* (qv) (Athlone), *Grogan's* (at Glasson).

See also: Lough Ree, 'the geographic centre of Ireland' - ask for directions!

ANTIQUE TAVERN

Slaney Street, Enniscorthy, Co Wexford
Tel: 054 33428

The delights of Enniscorthy include a superb location on the River Slaney, many memories of its historic past, a clutch of potteries, the annual Strawberry Fair and the *Antique Tavern*. This pub oozes atmosphere and it starts with your first view of it on its perch in Slaney Street. The pleasing black and white facade with the two-storied roof garden give promise of further attractions inside. And there are many. A small L-shaped bar serves a room full of interest with antique weapons, old prints of the town and a rake of press cuttings mainly in praise of the *Antique Tavern*.

This is a very friendly pub where the locals and the staff make visitors most welcome. Two businessmen drop in for a mid-morning cup of coffee and within minutes a stranger will be discussing with them the prospects for the All Ireland Hurling Championship or Ireland's chances of gold medals in the Olympic Games. Or maybe just the weather. It has won a number of 'pub of the year' prizes. Tourism is encouraged with a display of leaflets mainly about the town and County Wexford. Good food is available here with home-made soups and made to order sandwiches.

Try also: *Cronin's*, opposite, and *Cogan's* on Templeshannon quay.

See also: Vinegar Hill (site of the last battle of 1798), St Aidan's Cathedral and the Strawberry Fair in late June and early July.

PADDY BLUES

North Parade, Gorey, Wexford
Tel: 055 21133

'You can't miss it, it's blue all over,' I was told when I enquired as to where I might find this quaintly named pub. I found it in North Parade which, for the record, is at the south end of the town and the name - *Paddy Blues* - comes from the present owner's father, a Gorey cattle dealer who acquired the nickname. So blue it is on the outside and enigmatic it is inside. The character of the pub comes from the cheerful and slightly eccentric man who runs it - Pat Redmond. All around can be seen examples of his personality - lots of bric-a-brac, even calling it 'tat' would not be offensive - including old enamel trade signs, an amazing mix of old photographs, musical instruments and a pair of handpumps which are sadly not in use. Open fires add to the atmosphere and agreeable nature of this pub. A beer garden is a welcome sun trap in summer. Music is a regular feature of Sunday evenings but there are occasional and impromptu sessions at other times.

Gorey is a pleasant market town with a broad sweeping main street on the main N11 road from Dublin to Wexford Town. It is of great historic interest particularly for its part in the 1798 insurgence. Nearby are several pleasant seaside resorts and inland are the foothills of the Wicklow mountains.

Try also: *The Celtic Arms* at Ferns and *Kitty's* at Arklow (qv).

See also: Courtown harbour, Ferns Castle.

THE CAPE

Bull Ring, Wexford Town, Co Wexford
Tel: 053 22949

The major event of the year in Wexford is the Opera Festival in the late Autumn which lasts for three weeks and is often the scene for rarely performed operatic works. Finding accommodation during that period may be difficult but the pubs, whilst busy, are always welcoming, then and through the rest of the year. It's particularly so at *The Cape*, Eddie Macken's pub on the Bull Ring in the centre of town. This was once the venue for the so-called sport of bull baiting which was declared illegal centuries ago. It is also the location of a fine bronze statue of an Irish pikeman as a memorial to the 1798 rising. Another statue of note is that of John Barry the founder of the United States Navy who was born a few miles from Wexford. *The Cape* is one of those quintessential Irish pubs which serves a community with most of its needs; here it is bar, grocery and undertaker and also an off licence. This is a popular local pub but one which the visitor to Wexford should seek out. The quality of its stout is indicated by the number of regulars who await the opening of the bar each day.

Try also: *Bohemian Girl*, *White's Hotel*, *Hanrahan's* (New Ross).

See also: Irish National Heritage Park, Maritime Museum.

KITTY'S

Main Street, Arklow, Co Wicklow

First impressions of this large, slightly shadowy but very welcoming pub are of wood, wood and wood. Walls, ceiling, floors, bar, tables, chairs are all of wood. The large lounge to the right of the entrance is the popular place to be. The high bar is flanked by tall stools and large tables are fed by raffia backed chairs. Wooden stout barrels (more properly hogsheads, a measure of 54 gallons) are used for lamp supports and for standing customers. The whole effect is most pleasing. To the left is a more basic room which copes with overflows or groups seeking a degree of privacy. And upstairs is the *Loft Restaurant* with its own bar, justifiably popular and generally busy. Seafood is to the fore of the menu along with some excellent Irish steaks. Bar food is also available.

Kitty's is on the road that leads to the strands and the harbour. Arklow, which stands at the mouth of the River Avoca, has some splendid beaches and it is a town with lots of historical interest. *Gipsy Moth III*, the yacht in which Francis Chichester circumnavigated the world was built in the shipyard here and the town is also famous for its pottery products.

Try also: *The Meetings* near Avoca, *Cartoon Inn*, Rathdrum (qv).

See also: The Vale of Avoca and the Meeting of the Waters.

HARBOUR BAR

On the harbour side, in the centre of Bray, Co Wicklow

Bray is one of the best-established seaside resorts in Ireland with its dominating mound of Bray Head to the south and the Wicklow mountains forming a backdrop to a mile long beach and spacious strand. The town is at the southern end of DART, the fast electric train service through Dublin to Howth in the north and convenient for both the capital and the wonderful countryside around. *The Harbour Bar* is well situated in the centre of Bray and attracts many visitors as well as its coterie of regulars. It is a lively pub in which there are a number of small cosy rooms, all well decorated with some interesting artefacts, mainly nautical but including the stuffed head of a moose. There are open fires when required and an air of friendly cosiness. The Guinness is excellent. The O'Toole brothers who run the bar are justly proud of the place and of their excellent staff. They point back to its origins in 1831 which just about dates the beginnings of seaside holidays in the British Isles.

Try also: *Roundwood Inn* (qv), *The Queens* (Dalkey).

See also: Bray Head, Powerscourt Gardens and waterfall.

CARTOON INN

Main Street, Rathdrum, Co Wicklow
Tel: 0404 46774

And now for something completely different. Rathdrum, which is well known as the home of Charles Stewart Parnell, is also the base of the International Cartoon Festival which started in 1991 and is now held regularly over the first weekend in June, an Irish public holiday. Cartoonists from all over the world congregate and it is a great occasion.

In the town's main square is a pub with a sense of humour or more properly, a licensee with a sense of humour. The present owner of the *Cartoon Inn*, Peter King, with the help of local artist Terry Willers, devised the idea in which most of the walls of the bars of this jolly pub are covered with cartoons and then partially overlaid with framed examples of the same genre, some of which are for sale. The topics range from political to sporting, from world affairs to local matters and many famous folk are lampooned in them. During the festival it is, needless to say, very busy. And rightly so.

It has two bars on different levels with a mezzanine for the 'can't quite make my mind up' drinkers. Food is on sale at lunchtimes with bar snacks in the early evenings. There is a gaily decorated yard at the back for sunny day drinking and also a whitewashed wall bar which is available for private parties.

Try also: *The Meetings* near Avoca, *Old Court Inn* at Wicklow Town (qv).

See also: The Meeting of the Waters, Parnell's home at Avondale and the Forest Park.

THE ROUNDWOOD INN

In the village of Roundwood, Co Wicklow
Tel: 01 818107

Roundwood is one of Ireland's prettiest villages and the highest settlement in the Wicklow Hills. The views are fabulous and the scenery is spectacular. Jurgen and Aine Schwalm run this mid-eighteenth century former coaching inn with some style. Food and drink in the bar are served every day from 12 noon until 10 pm. The excellent restaurant has restricted opening hours and as it is advisable to book, phoning in advance will give you the up-to-date times. In 1995 it was honoured with the Egon Ronay Bar Food of the Year Award. The use of local produce brings such dishes as rack of Wicklow lamb and roast wild Wicklow venison to the table along with some Germanic specialities such as wiener schnitzel. There is an excellent wine list with bottles priced from around £10 to as much as £400 for a 1967 Pauillac! And Jurgen is proud of the quality of the Guinness in the bar. Polished wooden floors, stylish furniture, carefully chosen decor and open fires all add to a wonderful culinary experience. Enjoy it.

Try also: *Harbour Bar* at Bray (qv).

See also; Glendalough monastery, Russborough House.

OLD COURT INN

Court House Square, Wicklow Town
Tel: 0404 67680

You are left in no doubt about your drinking status in the *Old Court Inn*. A set of miniature traffic lights tells you: Green, the bar is open so carry on drinking; Amber: Last orders have been called so buy your final drink now, and Red: the bar is closed, sorry, see you tomorrow. It is just one feature of this prizewinning pub in a quiet corner of Wicklow Town. It stands opposite the handsome old court house and the jail which has been restored as a museum, and in front of the Billy Byrne monument which is a memorial to the men who fought for Ireland's freedom over the centuries.

The pub is good looking both out and in with a split level three sided bar. There are alcoves to eat and drink in and tall stools at the bar. The walls display many awards, some amusing legal cartoons and old prints and photographs of Wicklow. There are turf fires when needed and a resident pianist plays at weekends. The food and drink here is excellent. There is an emphasis on seafood and other local produce and three stouts are on sale. This is a most welcoming house.

Try also: *Bridge Tavern* in Wicklow Town, *Hunters Inn*, Rathnew, *Wicklow Arms*, Delgany.

See also: The Black Castle; Wicklow Regatta in early August.

HOUSE OF MCDONNELL

Castle Street in the centre of Ballycastle, Co Antrim
Tel: 012657 62975

The pub was built in 1744 and has remained in the McDonnell family ever since although it is now on the distaff side with the O'Neills as the present owners. This is a listed building and the interior is wonderfully ornate with its period as a spirit grocer up to 1921 clear to see. There are some splendid mirrors advertising whiskeys from Bushmills to Wilson's of Belfast. This is a welcoming and very comfortable pub and its facilities include an attractive beer garden and weekend music sessions through the year. Ballycastle is a fine town set inland but with resort facilities a mile away by the sea. It is in some of the most beautiful scenery of Northern Ireland and close to the Giant's Causeway. The famous Oul' Lammas Fair is held here every August with its horse trading and street theatre and general merrymaking.

Try also: *The Antrim Arms* and the *Boyd Arms* and the *Open Door* bakery opposite.

See also: the Antrim coast with the Giant's Causeway and the Carrick-a-Rede rope bridge.

BUSHMILLS INN

*On the Main Street of Bushmills, Co Antrim
Tel: 012657 32339*

The Bushmills Inn is in the village that is home to the world's oldest distillery still in business. They have been producing top-class legal whiskey at Bushmills since 1608 and a visit there is an essential part of any stay in the area. The inn dates from the 1830s when it was a coaching inn called the *Antrim Arms,* but it suffered the fate of many such establishments as the railway system developed. Its rebirth dates from 1987 when the present owners arrived. The restoration has been wonderful, producing a very welcoming and traditional pub with open peat fires, gas lighting and comfortable lounges and bars. There are eleven bedrooms, an oak-beamed loft, a circular library with an intriguing secret room and a garden patio. A double staircase leads to a pine-panelled gallery where paintings of the area by a local artist are displayed. *The Bushmills Inn* has won a number of awards including the prestigious British Airways Tourism Award which led to it being chosen as the venue for a trans-Atlantic television link-up on Saint Patrick's Day.

Try also: The tiny *McBride's Bar* in Lisnagunogue.

See also: Old Bushmills Distillery, and the Giant's Causeway.

LONDONDERRY ARMS

In the centre of the village of Carnlough, Co Antrim
Tel: 01574 85255

The Londonderry Arms has great charm and character and offers first-class service in all it sets out to do. Its situation is perfect in the attractive fishing village of Carnlough on the Antrim coast and it is an ideal spot from which to explore the nine glens of Antrim. There are 21 bedrooms and an award winning restaurant which has a reputation for rich home-made wheaten bread. The pleasant Arkle bar remembers one of the greatest steeplechasers of all times by a large painting of the horse that was presented to the hotel by its jockey Pat Taffe. The bar has a wide range of single malt whiskies.

It was built as a coaching inn in 1848 by the Marchioness of Londonderry and today retains that function with 21 bedrooms. It passed down the family until it came to her great grandson, Winston Churchill, in 1921. Even at that stage he was an established politician. He sold it in the late 1920s and for more than fifty years it has been in the hands of the present owners, the O'Neill family.

Try also: *The Waterfall.*

See also: Glencoy and Glenarrif.

WHITTLEY'S

401 Ballyclare Road, (B56), three miles NW of Glengormley, Co Antrim
Tel: 01232 832438

This pub has had more addresses than the British Royal family. It is in the townland of King's Moss which is often given as its location and its official address is Newtonabbey, for that is the district of County Antrim into which it falls. But Glengormley is as good a place to start to find it and when you do you will be well satisfied. There is a most welcoming and cosy public bar with open fires and a stone floor; a comfortable lounge and a well provided games room. The latest acquisition is a restaurant with a railway theme called The Signal Box and named after one that stood at the nearby level crossing but which has since been demolished . William Whittley built the *King's Moss Tavern* in 1840. He had previously traded as a spirit grocer in nearby Ballycraigy on Lord Donegal's estate but moved to King's Moss when the Earl of Shaftesbury, the reformer, married one of Donegal's daughters and would have opposed a spirit licence on the land. To date seven generations of Whittleys have lived here. The signal box may have gone but the railway remains and is often used for steam train excursions which are a guarantee to fill the restaurant. The food is first rate and traditional beer is served alongside some excellent draught Guinness.

Try also: *Crown and Shamrock* at Ballyvessey.

See also: Bellevue and the Belfast Zoological Gardens.

CROSSKEYS INN

42 Grange Road, Toome, Co Antrim - halfway between Randalstown and Portglenone on the B 52 road.
Tel: 01648 50694

According to J J Tohill in his guide *Pubs of the North* the *Crosskeys* 'is one of the most famous pubs in this land'. And the *Good Beer Guide* says: 'miss this and you miss history'. It is L-shaped, thatched, has white-washed walls, a beer garden, disabled access and a quiet room with a turf fire. It is also a listed building and probably dates from the seventeenth century. That is simply a list of its obvious attributes but the real qualities of the Crosskeys lie in its personality and character. The tap room is full of curios ranging from ancient notices to a tobacco twist guillotine and from a wooden arm that belonged to a sea captain to a gallery of local artists. The 'big room' where wonderful music sessions take place is filled with a unique collection of oil lamps, and the kitchen (which has its own bar) is the home for many beautiful ornaments. Traditional beer, usually Draught Bass, is often served here.

Try also: *O'Kane's* of Randalstown.

See also: Lough Neagh, the largest lake in the British Isles.

CROWN LIQUOR SALOONS

Great Victoria Street, Belfast
Tel: 01232 49476

This is one of the best known and best loved pubs in Ireland. *The
Crown*, which stands at the start of Belfast's famous 'Golden Mile'
pub crawl, is owned by the National Trust and managed for them by
Bass Ireland. It was built in 1826 as the Railway Tavern to service
the fledgling Belfast to Lisburn line and stood opposite the Great
Northern station. Now its neighbours are the *Europa Hotel* and the
Grand Opera House. Its new name came in 1885 when it was rebuilt
to the design of the owner's son by Italian craftsmen who were in
Belfast to build churches. And a century later the Trust gave it a
sympathetic restoration to its present glory. John Betjeman tagged it
'a many-coloured cavern' and his description is easy to understand.
Take your time to admire it from the tiled exterior with its ornate
columns and splendid iron gates to the magnificent bar with its
glorious tiled backdrop that faces ten private snugs or 'confessionals'
as they are called, where business deals, lovers' trysts or just good
ordinary conversation takes place. *The Crown* is one of the great gin
palaces of the world, a wonderful pub with many virtues: the mosaic
floor, the multi-coloured ceiling, stained and etched glass, luxurious
wall drapings, and richly coloured and carved wood screens. It
carries a fine selection of beers (including Draught Bass), wines and
spirits and the food has a high reputation. *The Crown* saw through
the Troubles with a few scars yet many famous folk continued to
come; so ask to see the visitors' book just to find out who they were.

Try also: *Robinson's* and *The Beaten Docket*.

See also: City Hall, Grand Opera House.

KELLY'S CELLARS

30 Bank Street, just off Royal Avenue in the centre of Belfast
Tel: 01232 324835

There are two ways of capturing the magic of *Kelly's Cellars.* You can go there, as I did. Or you can read the five pages that J J Tohill devotes to it in his book *Pubs of the North,* as I also did. He ought to know for his father owned the place for twenty years and it is clearly etched deep into his memory. The essentials are that it was built in 1720 and is the oldest continuously licensed premises in Belfast. It has a wealth of history and played its part in the 1798 insurrection when men like Wolfe Tone, Thomas Russell and Henry Joy McCracken met and plotted here. McCracken escaped from the redcoats by hiding under the bar. The Ulster novelist Hugh MacCartan described it as 'a compromise between a farmhouse and a bonded store.' One manager, Wee Joe Devlin went on to represent West Belfast in the nationalist cause at both Stormont and Westminster. Famous visitors abound, particularly sportsmen. From golf there have been Dai Rees the winning Ryder Cup captain and Fred Daly the only Irishman ever to win the Open Championship; boxers such as Floyd Patterson and Sonny Liston; and great footballers Matt Busby, Bill Shankley and Stanley Matthews along with the rest of the Blackpool team that won the 1953 FA Cup. There were entertainers too: Wilfred Pickles, G H Elliott, Sir John Martin

Harvey, Guy Mitchell and Buck Alec who signed himself as 'the world's greatest lion tamer.' Today's customers are journalists and lawyers and 'the plain people of Ireland'. There have been changes over the years at *Kelly's Cellars* but the essential atmosphere remains along with the barrel seats, whitewashed walls and archways as old as the pub. It is a listed building and drastic alterations are not possible; not that anyone would want to make them. Food is available at lunchtimes with a basic menu downstairs and more variety on the first floor. There is music, either traditional or blues, at the weekends when a later opening is allowed.

Try also: *Crown Liquor Saloons* (qv), *Kitchen Bar* (qv).

See also: Royal Avenue, the city's premier shopping street.

KINGS HEAD

829 Lisburn Road, Balmoral, Belfast
Tel: 01232 667805

This is a new pub in an old building. It dates from 1868 when it was
built for the use of senior managers of the Great Northern Railway -
Balmoral station is next door. The present licence dates from 1984
and the pub is owned by Tony Devlin and David Donnelly who did a
similar transformation with the Linen Hall in the city centre three
years before. At the *Kings Arms* there are several rooms including a
modern extension which is used for music - at weekends the pub is
open later than usual. The former library of the house has been
retained and still houses more than 1,000 books. It is a magnificent
room with quality furniture and all the ambience of a London club.
The other rooms have also retained their original fittings, panelling
and fireplaces; they are comfortable and stylish and include a tiled
parlour from where meals are served. The food here is substantial
and reasonably priced and there is a good selection of drinks
including the ubiquitous stout and a range of cask conditioned beers
such as Theakston Best Bitter, Younger's No 3 and Worthington
Best. The name incidentally stems from the fact that the Kings Hall -
famed in the past for championship boxing bouts - lies opposite.

See also: Kings Hall for superstar pop concerts and Balmoral golf
course.

KITCHEN BAR (CATNEY'S)

16 Victoria Square, Belfast
Tel: 01232 324901

This cosy and much loved pub dates from 1859; before that it was a boarding house for young ladies working at a nearby department store. For its first 130 years in business it was run by the Conlon family who created a famous relationship between the pub and the Empire Theatre which stood next door. Many famous stars trod its boards and the *Kitchen Bar* was the entertainers' pub. Charlie Chaplin appeared at the Empire as a young man, and so did Marie Lloyd, Lily Langtry, Will Fyffe, George Formby and many others. Ask the present owner, Pat Catney, to show you his collection of signed photographs and you will see a history of music hall. The walls of the pub are covered with theatre posters. The long narrow bar at the front is the popular place to be and the Parlour bar behind is a touch more up-market with many theatre memories on its walls. The food here is filling - good helpings of Irish stew for example - and there is a good choice of drinks. Pat serves cask beers from Scottish and Newcastle breweries and also guest ales from a 'cellar' that is two floors up. He runs regular beer festivals and his liking for real ales is such that he is contemplating building his own micro brewery.

Try also: *Kelly's Cellars* (qv), *Bittle's*, *Thompson's Garage* (it's a pub).

See also: St Anne's Cathedral, City Hall.

JENNY WATTS

High Street, Bangor, Co Down
Tel: 01247 270401

Bangor has something for everyone. It is in the view of many folk the best seaside resort in Northern Ireland with yachting, fishing, golf, bathing and some fine parks. Other places may disagree but they don't have *Jenny Watts*. This is a wonderful old pub, but more of that later. What of that name: who was she, this Jenny Watts? Various claims are made. One has it that she was a woman of noble birth wooed and chased by both a Gaelic chief and a Viking warrior; another says she was a smuggler, or an old hag who lived in a seaside cave. The most likely is that she took part in the rising of the United Irishmen in 1798. The one thing the legends have in common is that she drowned in the cave. And Jenny's cave is still there as one of Bangor's more bizarre landmarks.

This is the oldest pub in Bangor dating from 1780 (so Jenny might have known it) and it was formerly called *The Old House at Home*. The bar is wonderful; full of antiques and what must be the largest collection of pub mirrors in the province. There are many pictures too, so many in fact that a few are hung on the ceiling, and some unusual artefacts from the days that the pub was also a grocery. On the first floor, the restaurant is laid out as the former shop. There is also a patio which is much used on temperate days. The food here is highly praised at very reasonable prices with bar meals all day during the week. It is also one of that small but slowing growing band of Northern Ireland pubs that sell traditional beer. In this case Theakston Best Bitter from Yorkshire. Only live music is played here with jazz on Sunday lunchtimes and folk on Tuesdays.

Try also: *Bryansburn Inn*, *Windsor Bar*.

See also: Ulster Folk and Transport Museum, Bangor Castle.

HILLSIDE BAR

21 Main Street, Hillsborough, Co Down
Tel: 01846 682765

Hillsborough Castle was traditionally the residence of the Governor of Northern Ireland and the town has political importance. It is a pleasant town with some excellent pubs. *The Hillside Bar*, which is appropriately named, dates from 1777 although Diane Shields, the present owner, believes it may be earlier than that. There are three bars which contrast and attract differing groups of customers. The back bar is modern and popular with the younger set, whereas the smaller front bar is traditional with stone walls, flagged floors and an open fire. There is also a garden and an upstairs restaurant. *The Hillside* has picked up a few decorations in recent years including the Egon Ronay Irish Pub of the Year for 1995 and the Taste of Ulster award. Food is significant with bar meals all day and gourmet offerings in the restaurant. This is a real ale pub with draught beers from the Hilden brewery in nearby Lisburn, from Theakston (including the revered Old Peculier - note the spelling) and occasional guest ales from UK breweries. Guinness is well looked after and is available at both room temperature and chilled, a most unusual and commendable practice.

Try also: The *Plough Inn* (qv), *Marquis of Downshire*.

See also: The views from the fort, and take a peek at Government House.

PLOUGH INN

The Square (top of the hill) in Hillsborough, Co Down
Tel: 01846 682985

The Plough is another of Hillsborough's excellent pubs that also sells real ale - Theakston's Best Bitter. It is well situated in the centre of town and stands out as a elegant building of great antiquity - it dates from 1700. The public bar has roof timbers that are even older and were once in a London church. The lounge bar is two-level and at first glance appears to be like the owner's parlour which I suppose is really what it was in former days; hence the term 'public house'. Outstanding is a handsome fireplace and some fine furniture. Pictures of horses and equine artefacts dominate this pub; but not the hunters, rather the working shires of an Ulster farm. Upstairs is a wine bar and a restaurant presided over by the licensee, Derek Patterson, who finds time to write a food column for a local newspaper. The food could be nothing less than excellent and there is bar food all day, every day. *The Plough* is a comfortable and welcoming pub.

Try also: *Hillside Bar* (qv) and *The Marquis of Downshire Inn.* It was the first Marquis, with the family name of Hill (after whom the town was named), who invented the screw top bottle!

See also: the parish church and its two organs, Lagan Valley Country Park.

BEAR TAVERN

62 High Street, Holywood, Co Down
Tel: 01232 426837

Here is a pub that has maintained its place in the *Good Beer Guide* for six years making it one of the pioneers of real ale in Northern Ireland. Its original description of: 'long, narrow bar with handsome traditional interior, sloping stone floor, tiles, mahogany, cosy corners and lots of mirrors and glass,' cannot be bettered. The sloping floor intrigues as I imagine it is intended to. On the first floor of this lively pub is a comfortable lounge and a roof garden that is open in appropriate weather. There are open fires, no obtrusive music, bar food at lunchtimes and easy access for wheelchairs. Draught beers include McEwan's Eighty Shilling and Theakston Best Bitter. All in all this is a delightful pub that fits well into the small community of Holywood. This pleasant residential town stands on the south side of Belfast Lough between Belfast and Bangor. It boasts the only maypole in Northern Ireland alongside which is a statue of 'Johnny the Jig' playing his fiddle for the dancers.

Try also: *Seaside Tavern, Jenny Watts* (qv) in Bangor.

See also: Ulster Folk and Transport Museum, Crawfordsburn Country Park.

WHITE HORSE INN

49 Main Street, Saintfield, Co Down
Tel: 01238 510417

There is lots of quality in this pub which sits proudly on the small town's main thoroughfare. It is an appropriately named pub for inside you will find a dedication to horses (not particularly white ones) that would be hard to better. Not only is the tackle displayed but paintings, photographs and ornaments, and they relate to horses of all types - working, sporting, racing and pets. The present landlord's father was brought up working with horses and indeed this is horse territory.

There are three bars including the cellar bar which doubles as a restaurant in which they serve ostrich. 'It looks like fillet steak but tastes like duck,' according to Craig Spratt the landlord. It is imported from Zimbabwe and one recipe has it dressed with raspberry mint jelly. For those less adventurous there is a fine selection of sea food and some imaginative pies. There is also a special menu for children. The other bars are a mish mash of tiny rooms and snugs with privacy for those who want it and general comfort for all customers. One of the other great attractions is that traditional (real) ale is sold including Theakston Best Bitter from Yorkshire and occasional guest beers. There are no juke boxes or piped music, it is simply a pub where the art of conversation has not been lost.

Try also: *Rowallane Inn*, *Primrose Bar* in Ballynahinch.

See also: Rowallane Gardens, Castle Espie.

BLAKE'S OF THE HOLLOW

6 Church Street in the centre of Enniskillen, Co Fermanagh
Tel: 01365 322143

This is a pub with real character. It is a listed building both inside
and out and the obvious attractions of its red and black paintwork
positively draw you in to it. You will not be disappointed. A tiled
floor, wood lined walls, high stools at a marble topped bar with
pedestal lights behind which there are four large sherry casks, all
make for a place that oozes personality. The Herbert family bought it
in 1887 and tastefully 'modernised' it and nothing much has
changed since then apart from the building of toilets for ladies some
30 years ago. William Blake bought the pub in 1929 and now his
son Donal runs it. Arthur Blake runs the family's licensed restaurant
in Enniskillen and Joseph Blake is the company secretary. When
other members of the family are in town they help out in the pub.
But the star behind the bar is Michael who has the awesome
reputation of pulling the best pint of Guinness in Ulster. He signs
himself when doing this by placing a shamrock on the head of the
pint. He also brews up a bowl of soup that is revered throughout the
land. It is called Blakes of the Hollow to distinguish it from another
of the company pub's in the town.

Enniskillen is beautifully situated on the River Erne between the
Upper and Lower Loughs and is a cruising and angling centre.

Try also: *Blake's* in The Diamond, *Blake's* in Townhall Street

See also: Enniskillen Castle, Castle Coole (a National Trust
property).

GASLIGHT BAR

40 Loy Street, Cookstown, Co Tyrone
Tel: 016487 65640

The market town of Cookstown claims to have the longest and widest main street in the whole of Ireland. It is one and a half miles long, tree-lined and rather beautiful. It also has a lot of pubs from which the *Gaslight Bar* stands out as a fine example of how to restore an old pub without it losing any of its essential character. Its first licence was granted in 1839 when it was called *The Premier*. But *Gaslight Bar* it now is and gas lit it is, an unusual feature for a pub these days but how wonderfully atmospheric. This is a twin level bar with stone walls, open fires in attractive fire places, dark wood facings and bentwood furniture. There is a much used piano and music sessions of all types are held regularly. Cookstown is the home town of my dentist and he had me in the chair unable to speak when he recommended the *Gaslight Bar* to me. All I could do was nod agreement to him; I was glad I did.

Try also: *The Black Horse*, *The Dunleath*.

See also: Drum Manor Forest Park, Killymoon Castle, Tullaghoge Fort.

BREWERY AND DISTILLERY VISITOR CENTRES

BUNRATTY WINERY

Alongside the Bunratty Folk Park on the road to Sixmilebridge, Bunratty,
Co Clare
Tel: 061 362222

Visitors are shown how mead is made and are given a tasting. The winery is open every day from 10 am until 5.30 pm. Mead is an ancient wine with honey as its main ingredient and has a very romantic history - the term 'honeymoon' is said to derive from it. Bottles of mead may be purchased but not, unfortunately, bottles of *poitín* which is distilled here. For whilst this is the only legal *poitín* still in Ireland sadly the mystical spirit produced cannot be sold in the country except at duty free outlets. It is however exported widely to Britain, Europe and the United States. The history of *poitín* (which is the Irish spelling) is well told in *In Praise of Poteen* (which is how the English spell it) by John McGuffin.

BIDDY EARLY BREWERY

*In the centre of Inagh on the main road from Ennis to Ennistymon in
County Clare
Tel: 065 36742*

This is the first brewery in the Republic to produce cask conditioned
beers for many years. Black Biddy Stout was the first product of the
tiny brewery in the ground floor 'cellar' of this pleasant family-run
pub. Now others have joined it. Visitors are welcome to see round
the brewery but it is perhaps as well to ring the owner, Peadar
Garvey, in advance.

BEAMISH & CRAWFORD BREWERY

On South Main Street, in the centre of Cork City
Tel: 021 276841

The company have been in business for more than 200 years although there is evidence of brewing on the site since the early seventeenth century. There are no general visitor facilities though a limited number of parties are allowed to tour the brewery but only by prior written arrangement.

JAMESON IRISH WHISKEY HERITAGE CENTRE

In the centre of Midleton, 13 miles east of Cork on the main Waterford to Cork road (N25), in County Cork
Tel: 021 613594

The buildings of the old distillery have been brought back to life and there are guided tours daily from March to October between 10 am and 5 pm. The cost is £3.50 and this includes a good measure of your choice of whiskey. A lucky couple may get the chance of trying several. The world's largest pot still is on display as well as a 40-foot diameter water wheel and many other interesting artefacts. There is a small museum, souvenir shop and bar. The 12-year-old Distillery Reserve Whiskey can be bought here and nowhere else. Next door is the high-tech new distillery which opened in 1975 which also produces gin and vodka.

IRISH WHISKEY CORNER

Bow Street Distillery, Smithfield, Dublin 7
Tel: 01 8725566

In a corner of what was once a warehouse of Jameson's Dublin distillery is this fascinating museum and display of how Irish whiskey is made. It starts with a guided tour of the exhibit area, is followed by an audiovisual presentation and concludes with the opportunity to taste a selection of whiskeys from all over the world but in particular those from Ireland in the splendid Ball O'Malt bar. There is a tour on weekdays throughout the year at 5.30 pm. and extra ones in the summer months including weekends. The cost is £3. There is also a gift shop.

JAMESON'S LITERARY PUB CRAWLS

Starts at The Duke Pub, Duke Street, Dublin
Tel: 01 454 0228

The crawl begins at 7.30 pm every evening with additional ones at 12 noon on Sundays. A number of famous pubs are included, many of which are in this guide, and there are suitable breaks for refreshment and entertainment by the actor/guides. It is great fun. The crawl costs £6 or £5 for students and senior citizens. In *The Bailey Restaurant*, also in Duke Street, the front door of 7 Eccles Street the home of Leopold Bloom the hero of James Joyce's novel *Ulysses* can be found. Patrick Kavanagh declared it 'now shut'.

PORTER HOUSE BREWING COMPANY

The Porter House, Parliament Street, Dublin

See pub entry on page 51.

WORLD OF GUINNESS
EXHIBITION

Guinness Hop Store, Crane Street, Dublin 8
Tel: 01 4533645

This is one of the most popular tourist attractions in Ireland. Many thousands of visitors come each year to see the audiovisual presentation and the many artefacts of the brewing process that are displayed in the former hop store of the brewery. There are separate displays of the coopering process and of brewery transport. And each visitor is able to sample the famous black stout. There is a souvenir shop where copies of the famous Guinness advertising posters are on sale as well as other gifts. The exhibition is open from 10 am with the last admissions at 5.30 pm. and the cost is £2.

SMITHWICK'S BREWERY

St Francis Abbey Brewery, Kilkenny
Tel: 056 21014

Smithwick's is the oldest working brewery in Ireland dating from 1710. It is part of the Guinness Group but specialises in ales and lagers. The abbey of St Francis, which is a national monument, is in the grounds of the brewery which takes its name. There are no brewery visits but a video show followed by samples of the products takes place there from Monday to Friday during the months of June to September at 5 pm. Tickets can be obtained from the Kilkenny Tourist Office in Rose Inn Street. Admission is free but each visit is limited to 50 people.

LOCKE'S DISTILLERY MUSEUM

Kilbeggan, Co Westmeath
Tel: 0506 32134

This is a community based facility in the former Locke's distillery that ceased production in 1959 after 200 years. Visitors can either follow the whole process of distilling whiskey on a guided tour or find their own way round with the help of a leaflet. It is open from 9 am until 5 pm. from April to October and from 10 am to 5 pm. for the rest of the year. Admission charge is £2 with special rates for groups. There is a bar which sells all the group's whiskeys, a cafe and a souvenir shop.

OLD BUSHMILLS
DISTILLERY COMPANY

Bushmills, Co Antrim. It is 55 miles north west of Belfast.
Tel: 012657 31521

Visitors are welcome to join tours of not only Ireland's but the world's oldest licensed distillery on all weekdays through the year. They are on mornings and afternoons from Monday to Thursday and on Friday mornings. There are some extra tours in summer and it is best to phone in advance. The cost is £2 . After the tour visitors are given a dram of their choice in the distillery museum which could include the 10-year-old single malt or the famed Black Bush. The distillery dates from 1608 although there is evidence that whiskey may have been made there in the thirteenth century. Accommodation and meals are available at the *Bushmills Inn* (qv).

HILDEN BREWERY AND VISITOR CENTRE

Hilden House, Grand Street, Hilden, Lisburn, Co Antrim
Tel: 01846 663863

The second largest brewery in Northern Ireland was born in 1981 and produces only traditional beers from its 15-barrel plant in the former stables of a Georgian country house. It now has a visitor centre and museum and also a restaurant. Visitors are welcome at most reasonable times. The cost is £3 which includes two pints of beer.

BASS ULSTER BREWERY VISITOR CENTRE

Glen Road, Belfast 11
Tel: 01232 301301

Visits to the brewery's new visitor centre need to be booked in advance with the Public Relations Department (Telephone extension 2220) and are only available for organised parties. The brewery produces a wide range of beers including the popular Caffrey's Irish Ale and several beers for other brewers.

OTHER BREWERIES AND DISTILLERIES

Cherry Brothers Ltd, New Ross, County Waterford

Irish Brewing Co, Newbridge, County Kildare

Macardle, Moore, Dundalk, County Louth

James J Murphy & Co, Ladyswell Brewery, Cork City

Cooley Distillery, Dundalk, County Louth

Bass Ulster Brewery Visitor Centre

SLÁINTE

Health and long life to you
Land without rent to you
The partner of your choice to you
A child every year to you
and may you be half an hour in heaven
before the devil knows you're dead

INDEX